**Ireland's greatest son —
Scotland's founding father**

The magnificent Gael

by Reginald B. Hale
FSA Scot

Printed by
MOM Printing Ltd.
Ottawa

In Memory of
my great-uncle

WILSON CARLILE C.H., D.D.
Founder of the Church Army

He was descended
from the
Kindred of St. Columba
and like Columba, he gave up
wealth and position to take the
love of God to the deprived,
the unwanted and
outcast.

AUTHOR:

Editor, artist, historian Reginald Britten Hale has spent his life in journalism. In World War II he served in Europe with the USAAF and was awarded the Bronze Star Medal. For seven years he was Editor of NEW WORLD NEWS, a global magazine printed in 24 languages. Retired, he now lives in Ottawa, Canada, engaged in studies of Celtic history. He is a Fellow of the Celtic Chair of the University of Ottawa.

FOREWORD

By the Very Rev. Lord MacLeod of Fuinary, Founder of the Iona Community, Iona, Scotland.

"It takes a distance to get a proper focus. Reginald Hale from Canada has seen St. Columba in better perspective than most historians closer at hand.

"As one who for nearly forty years busied myself with Columba's isle of Iona, I have seen and studied most biographies of the saint, ancient and modern. No other biography I have seen has caught, in such concise compass and with such warmth of appreciation, the true image of the saint.

"Nor is his work simply archaic recovery. To a most remarkable degree St. Columba speaks to our day. May many historians reach out for it and ponder the present in the light of what turns out to be by no means passed."

SOME LEADING PERSONALITIES

This book enters a period of history, which to many, is not well known. The time of turmoil as the Roman Empire crumbled before wave after wave of roving tribes from the East. Law and loyalties eroded and beliefs withered.

It may be helpful to introduce some of the leading personalities who contended with the problems of this dark age.

NIALL-of the Nine Hostages, High King of Ireland about 400 AD. His raiders kidnapped a Roman-Briton who became **Patrick,** Patron Saint of Ireland. He converted Niall's sons including **Conall Gulban** king of Donegal, the great-grandfather of **St. Columba.**

Magnus Maximus, Roman commander of Britain, drove off attacks by Picts, Irish and Saxons. The Legions at York proclaimed him Emperor in 383. He led them to Gaul to resist the Goths and Franks and died in 388.

Cunedda, one of his officers, led an army of Britons to Wales and drove out the Irish invaders. He founded the kingdom and dynasty of Gwynedd.

Bishop Germanus of Auxerre, sent by the Pope to counter the Pelagian heresy among the Britons, raised the morale and discipline of the British troops who defeated the Picts and Saxons at the Alleluia Victory in 429.

Vortigern, governor of Britain, recruited Saxon mercenaries **Hengist** and **Horsa** in 444 to defend against attacks of the Picts. He himself fell under Hengist's control.

Martin, Patron Saint of France, was a Roman cavalry officer who became a monk and founded the first monastery in France, 372 at Tours. He trained and sent out missionaries to Christianize the pagan country folk of Gaul.

Ninian, a Briton trained by St. Martin, founded a monastery called Candida Casa at Whithorn in south-west Scotland that spread the Faith among the Picts and Irish.

Arthur, Battle Commander of the Christian Britons, fought and won 12 battles against the pagan invaders. The decisive victory at Mount Badon in 516 won peace for 20 years. But in 537 rebellious Britons allied with pagan Picts defeated and killed Arthur at the battle of Camlann.

This disaster led to an aggressive revival of paganism that nearly wiped out Christianity in Britain and Ireland. This book follows the course of this homeric struggle and of the men who decided its outcome. Especially the Irish prince **Columcille** or **Columba.**

TABLE OF CONTENTS

Photos & illustrations by R.B. Hale
Cover Lettering by Eileen Richardson
Lettering of Poem p. 170 by Karen Bailey

INTRODUCTION

The Dark Ages, roughly between 400 and 1000 AD, are sometimes thought of as an historical quaking bog between the sure footing of Roman times and the firm ground of the Norman period. In Britain there were indeed dark times during those centuries, though perhaps they seem dim because of a long-held belief that nothing of interest happened in Britain before 1066.

This is not so. Three of the most momentous decisions in the history of Britain were made during those centuries.

First, the racial stock of the British was decided: basically English but with a surprisingly large intermix of Celtic blood. Second, the language of the nation was decided: English became the common tongue but was constantly enriched by others, Britonic, Latin, Norse, French and many more. It is an inclusive language.

After 400 AD the light that had shone from Imperial Rome guttered low and the Britons stumbled along in the gloom of uncertainty, bedevilled by waves of unwelcome invaders.

"What was is past: what comes is not yet born.

We stand in the quiet hours of dark before the dawn."

Yet darkness never wholly triumphed. Already light was streaking the western horizon. For while this age was dark in Britain, in Ireland it was becoming a shining period, of noble art, brilliant intellects and bold spirits — the Irish Golden Age.

As this illumination spread forth from Ireland, it brought about the third vital decision for Britain, the most far-reaching of them all. The Faith of the British people was decided. They, like the Irish, became rooted in Christianity. From this spiritual watershed has flowed the ideals and philosophy of the race, its home life and public festivals, its culture, music and art, its education — and sense of humour. Its concepts of law, of service and freedom — in fact, the whole distinctive civilization that the Britons and the Irish have exported to the world, moulding the histories of Canada, America, Australia and wherever the four winds have blown them.

It was not an inevitable decision. Many areas such as Asia Minor and North Africa which once were Christian, are no longer so. In Britain itself the outcome was in flux for five centuries until at last the tide turned and the decision became irrevocable. At the place where the tide turned we meet St. Columba of Iona, affectionately known to the Irish as Columcille. His life was a decisive factor in the turning of the tide.

Columcille was a Celt, a Gael of Ireland, and his story takes us back into the world of our Celtic heritage. We English-speaking peoples are far more Celtic than perhaps most of us realize. A large percentage of native Britons mixed with the English settlers by intermarriage and employment. They adopted the English tongue but their blood remained Celtic. Numbers of Bretons came to Britain with the Norman conquerors, one most famous Breton family being the Royal Stewarts. After the heavy mortality of the Black Death in 1349, many Bretons and Irish came over to fill up the work force or obtain empty land. When the Tudor Kings came to the Throne of England numerous Welsh followed them. In the same way, waves of Scots came south with the Stuart Kings. There can be few families in the British Isles who do not have some Celtic blood. So the story of the Celts is our common heritage. And let us recall that it was the Celts who made for Britain that vital third decision of Faith.

Gaelic words, used to describe Celtic concepts or customs, in this book are set in italics and will remind us that Gaelic was Columcille's own language, that poetic tongue that was ancient before English, French or German ever took form.

Special problems arise when writing about "the Dark Ages". Records were few, myths were many and methods of dating in transition. Learned scholars sincerely disagree about most events and every date is in dispute. Happily great strides have recently been made in Celtic studies and knowledge about this period has more than doubled in the last twenty years. Those of us who are not professional historians can now find excellent new books to throw light on this age. Some most informative ones are named in the Bibliography at the end of the book. I gratefully acknowledge my debt to the authors.

New discoveries are always being made and no writer can feel sure that he has marshalled all the facts or interpreted them wholly correctly. Like a witness in Court he must aim to "tell the truth, the whole truth and nothing but the truth." Yet the best he can do is to present the evidence as he sees it.

In the story of Columcille there are so few incontrovertible facts. Yet it would be tedious to the reader to hedge every sentence with "it is believed", "maybe", "possibly".

If such words are used sparingly it is from a wish to make the text readable, but with no desire to be dogmatic.

The Sixth Century when Columcille lived may seem remote yet the conditions of his world were strikingly like our own. Then too a great world system, which for centuries had given intellectual and political stability, had broken down. Social and legal guidelines were gone and men's loyalties were confused. Life's only aim seemed to be riches and power, violence the accepted method of amassing them.

Columcille, who was born to wealth and power, chose to march in a totally opposite direction. By the example of his life he set the people of Ireland and Britain on a course which led them to a new civilization. What he did, why and how he did it are relevant studies for today. This book is written in the hope of introducing historically minded readers to a fascinating, formative period.

I owe a special debt of gratitude to Judge John R. Matheson and Dr. Margaret W. Labarge of Ottawa, Father Leonard E. Boyle, O.P., Brother Edmund Kiely, CFC of Iona College, N.Y., Archibald Hutchison, historian and poet of Glasgow, Wallace Clark, the sailor-author of Ulster. Their help has been unfailing.

OTTAWA, Canada   Reginald B. Hale.

Origins

Celtic Warrior's Shield — first century A.D. At British Museum.

St. Patrick's Bell — fifth century A.D. At National Museum of Ireland.

We headed into the Donegal mountains along lanes too small to be shown on our tourist map of Ireland. Ahead the waters of Lough Gartan glinted through the spring leaves and cloud shadows chased the few patches of sunshine off the hillsides.

"It can't be far now", I said. We stopped to ask the way from some children dawdling home from school, satchel on back. "Up to the top of the hill and you'll not be able to miss it". But of course we did. So we asked a farmer coming from his henhouse, holding in his cap a clutch of warm eggs. "Back to the lodge gates, then up the drive and turn left on the cart track." At the end of the track we found what we were looking for.

My wife and I had come a long way from our home in Canada to stand here. Not much to see really, only a rectangle of boulders, "the flagstone of Rath Cro". Violets and primroses were blooming in the rank grass which grew between the rocks, giving them a festive air. At this remote spot on Thursday 7th December 521 AD a child was born on this "birthing stone" who is known to history as St. Columba of Iona — or Columcille as the Irish call him. We will use both names.†

We had searched in many books to learn about this man, in old books and in new ones, written by his friends or by writers who were less friendly. Now our card index files bulged with data. But to know a mass of facts about a man is not the same as knowing him as a person. So in the hope of learning to know him in a personal way we travelled to the places which had been familiar to him, the glens and the islands of Ireland and Scotland. Here we might bridge the separating gulf of fourteen hundred years.

This man holds a unique place in Irish and British history because he is the first really historical character of our race, our first knowable ancestor.

Before Columcille the Dark Ages were dark indeed and semi-mythical figures moved like wraiths in the gloom and no one can tell whether they were flesh or fable. Then suddenly the dawn light touches the figure of a man who stands forth real and recognizable — Columcille of Iona.

Many a hero before his day was memorialized by the bards in song and legend but with oft-telling their deeds waxed ever more fantastic until, moulded into demi-gods, they lost all human likeness. This fate befell the British hero Arthur, who is thought to have been living when Columcille was born. Although his fame has reached Hollywood, erudite scholars still debate whether historically he ever existed at all.

What circumstances made it possible for Columcille to break out of the darkness of myths into the light of fact? Why is he an historical figure while Arthur dwells in fairyland?

The explanation lies in the Latin tag, "Scripta manent" — what is written survives. Columcille did so much to spread the skill of writing that it seems fitting that his memory is the first to benefit from a written record. By studying the writings of men who lived close to his times we can today judge, to some extent, what is fact and what is fable. They tell us what he looked like, we can read his actual words, almost hear his voice and look into his face.

It was a wee, wailing face which saw its first Irish dawn at Gartan that Thursday in 521 but his mother Eithne thought him a beautiful baby and like all young mothers, imagined great things lay in store for her first-born son. In a dream she had received an exquisite robe, bright with the colours of all the wild flowers, but the wind had swirled it away and it grew and spread out until it covered the mountains and islands.

Eithne came of the royal line of Leinster kings. Her husband Felim macFergus was a chieftain of the dynastic family of Ui Neill, heirs of the mighty Niall-of-the-Nine Hostages, High King of Ireland. So their little son was born a prince of the Blood Royal and would inevitably live his life in the glare of the political limelight. His parents had every reason to hope that someday he might hold the sceptre of the High King and reign at Tara.

But the child also had another heritage. His great-great-grandfather Niall had been a heathen and an unabashed slave raider. However several of his sons had been con-verted by St. Patrick, the ex-slave who brought Christianity to the Irish. One of these sons was Conall Gulben, king of Donegal. St. Patrick with his staff marked a cross on King Conall's shield and from then on his descendants took as their symbol a Hand grasping a Cross. From the time of his conversion his clan had been staunch for the Faith. So it was that Felim macFergus, grandson of Conall, was himself a deacon of the Church and his son was born into a devout Christian family.

His father's mother was said to have been Eirc, daughter of Lorn macErc, a fact which profoundly influenced the geography of Columba's life. Lorn was a prince of Dal-riada, now a part of County Antrim. His people had been squeezed uncomfortably into the north-east corner of Ulster by the expanding power of the Northern Ui Neill and about 500 AD he and his brothers decided to emigrate to a less crowded land. The brothers Lorn, Fergus and Angus led an expedition of 150 warriors across the sea to Alban, the north of Scotland. They established a settlement in Argyll around the rocky fortress of Dunadd.

As a child Fergus had been blessed by St. Patrick and the Dalriad colony was Christian from its beginning. When Lorn and Fergus died they received Christian burial on a small island called Iona. So it may have been a great-grandfather of Columcille who led the first Scots to establish a permanent home in Scotland.

Felim and Eithne took their child six miles to Kilmacrenan to be baptised by the priest Cruithnechan, which is pronounced "Crenan". He was christened Colum, which in Latin is Columba. He also received the traditional family name of Crimthann that means a fox, an animal admired by the Gaels.

The Irish Gaels had a custom of fosterage. Children of noble families as soon as weaned were placed with foster parents to be brought up and educated. It was not thought fitting for a noble's son to consort with his father until he had "taken arms" at the age of seventeen.

Felim chose as his son's foster father the priest Cruithnechan and Columcille spent his boyhood with him at Kilmacrenan beside the little Lannan river which runs down to join the salt ocean tides in Lough Swilly. When the priest was teaching him the alphabet he made the lesson more fun by marking the letters on a cake. As the boy ate the cake he learnt his ABC. When half the cake was eaten,

Colum paddled across to the opposite bank of the Lannan river and his foster father, on the alert for omens, predicted that he would spend half his life overseas.

A fine horseman and good at all sports, Colum specially excelled in handling boats and was happiest when afloat amid the roar of the waves. While quite young however he developed the habit of slipping away from the crowd to pray in the church. It earned him the nickname "Colum-cille" — church dove. Like most Gaelic nicknames, it was apt and stuck to him for life.

He grew into a tall, handsome youth, a classic example of the Gael, with a broad forehead, luminous grey eyes and thick blond hair of small curls. Perhaps he inherited the primrose-yellow hair of his formidable ancestor, Niall-of-the-Nine-Hostages. Good looks were important as the Irish only chose fine-looking men for their kings. He possessed a glorious singing voice of great volume but which never lost its clarity of tone, a useful asset in a society that rated music along with food and drink as one of the three necessities of life.

After leaving his foster father, Columcille continued his education with the two most learned teachers of his day, Bishop Finbar at Moville and St. Finian at Clonard. Both found him a brilliant student.†

As Columcille stepped into manhood the world was at his feet. With wealth and princely rank, brains and good looks, and behind him the most powerful dynastic family in Ireland who were setting high hopes upon him, power and fame were his for the taking and no ambition seemed beyond reach.

When he was just in his twenties the High King of Ireland died and it is probable that this was the first of two occasions on which tradition states he was put forward as claimant to the kingdom.

Columcille renounced the claim. He turned his back on all the bright prospects and struck out on a diametrically opposite course. Rich, he insisted on becoming poor. Royal, he chose to be a nobody. Powerful, he became the servant of others.

Pity his baffled elders whose hopes for him had been so high. What had come over him? Surely if he wished to serve God, there were large opportunities for doing good as High King. It was mad to cast away all his advantages. The road to Tara was open to him; if he chose, he could be monarch of Ireland.

Columcille chose another road and became instead the greatest son of Ireland of all time.

Chapter two

This promising young man, whose start in life looked so unpromising to his elders, is known to us chiefly through the writings of Adomnan macRonan (624-704), ninth Abbot of Iona. About 688 AD he wrote "The Life of St. Columba", incorporating in it an earlier life by the sixth Abbot Cummin the Fair. As a student Cummin had been taught by Columcille and he in his turn had taught Adomnan. Both were cousins belonging to Columcille's own clan.

This book is the first complete biography of post-Roman Europe and is unique, not only for so early a date, but for centuries to come. The oldest surviving copy, transcribed at Iona about 713, was taken to the Irish monastery at Reichenau in Austria where it was safe from the Vikings who devastated the libraries of Ireland. Now it is treasured at Schaffhausen, in Switzerland.†

Adomnan was a well-read, saintly man, a distinguished statesman of his own day and altogether a worthy biographer of his famous cousin. Dr. Kathleen Hughes of Cambridge called him, "A learned man with conscientious, scholarly standards." In his preface he stated, "Let no one suppose that I write falsehood or things doubtful, but what has come to my knowledge through tradition passed down by men who knew the facts and, after diligent inquiry, by hearing them from informed, trustworthy old men." Undoubtedly what he wrote was the truth as he and his contemporaries believed it a century after Columcille's death.

By a remarkable coincidence of history Adomnan,

Britain's first biographer, lived at the same time as the "father of English history", the Venerable Bede of Jarrow (673-735). They were personally acquainted because Adomnan visited Jarrow and Bede acknowledged his debt to Adomnan's scholarship.

"Church History of the English People", Bede's famous work, throws light on the century after Columcille. The historian of the Britons, St. Gildas, wrote his "Destruction of Britain" in about the year 560. These three authors, Adomnan, Bede and Gildas, are the basic sources for our study.

By and large, other mediaeval writings have to be treated with caution because the line between fact and fancy was so blurred and often a pagan folk tale was attached to the name of a popular saint. A ninth century scribe bewailed "the Irish habit of preferring fiction to true history." Dr. Ludwig Bieler described the average mediaeval Life of a saint as "a kind of religious romance. The author often wanted to propagate a cult or even support a temporal claim of the saint's church."†

Not till the nineteenth century did scholarly histories appear like the splendid studies of Bishop William Reeves and the "History of Celtic Scotland" by W.F. Skene, Historiographer-Royal for Scotland. In the last two decades Celtic studies have made rapid advances.

But as we return to Adomnan's book we must be warned that what he wrote was not history in the modern sense, but hagiogrpahy, the spiritual record of a saint. His book was an act of devotion to the founder of Iona and his aim was to show Columcille's sanctity, evidenced by miracles of God.

Historians are tempted to turn from such hagiography in exasperation but, as John M. Ross said, "It is easy to pronounce it a ludicrous fiction but no criticism would be more shallow. Adomnan's work is honest to the core, penetrated with devout sincerity". It is rich in historical clues although in searching for them we must make a clear distinction between magic and miracles. They are things of a totally different nature. Magic attempts to influence events by occult means or witchcraft. It is contrived by man. But miracles come only from the action of the Creator Himself.

Adomnan wrote about miracles and he was writing for clergy, men rooted in the Bible. So he told his story unadorned by the what-when-where details sought by modern historians. Columcille prayed: a amiracle happened. To Adomnan that was the heart of the story, indeed the whole story. Often he repeated the phrase, "Quid plura?" — "Why say more?" — and leaves us devoutly wishing he had said much more.

With such a wealth of sources to draw on, both old and new, it would seem a simple task to record a lifelike story of Columcille. "Why don't you tell it just the way it happened?" was the advice of one of our friends. So it comes as something of a shock to find so many contradictory opinions about him in recent books. At times it is hard to believe the authors are writing about the same man.

In a television travelogue about Scotland, while the camera scanned the isle and abbey of Iona, the commentator intoned, "Long ago a violent man came here seeking peace which he found at last upon this remote island." Is this really the story of Iona? Or is it just a popular myth?

This version however has appeared in books by historians of repute. John Prebble in *Lion of the North* wrote "Columba's hot blood was responsible for savage slaughter. Three thousand men died to prove he was no thief". The author of *The Highlands in History*, C.R. MacKinnon of Dunakin, quoted "a recent historian of the Church of Scotland has said probably no Christian priest, before the political Popes of the Middle Ages was ever responsible for so much bloodshed". *Everyman's Book of Saints* asserted, "While Columba was angry at the King's decision, he instigated war". In his *Historical St. Columba*, Dr. W. Douglas Simpson charged, "He was vindictive, often violently irascible... blinded by headstrong craving for revenge, he organized rebellion".

Columcille stands accused of grave crimes. Violence and revenge: rebellion and war: bloodshed and slaughter. "Such is the Columba of popular tradition", admitted Professor Skene, the greatest scholar of Scotland's Celtic past. "But it is based on very questionable statements which do not stand the test of critical examination".

Nevertheless criticisms made by historians of standing cannot be lightly ignored. For if Columcille was guilty of even half these crimes, he must have been a thoroughly bad man. Yet history recorded that the outcome of his life was reconciliation and the spread of faith and learning.

Something must be drastically wrong with the image of popular tradition. Figs do not grow on thistles. Rotten trees do not bear good fruit. There is no such thing as a "fig-bearing thistle". The question must be faced squarely. Thistle of fig-tree? Which was he?

Celts blowing the carnyx war trumpet.
Gundestrup cauldron.

Lia Fail — Stone of Destiny at Tara.

Loch Gartan, Donegal, where Columcille was born. Ruins of the Convent of St. Eithne, his mother.

The temptation is to plunge immediately into a discussion of the acts for which Columcille has been criticized. But this would be a mistake until his origins and background are understood and his acts can be judged in their proper setting. Many of the criticisms arise from ignorance of the culture and social conditions of his age. For instance, one author charged, "he intervened illegally in politics". This may seem valid, judged by the customs of the twenthieth century but judged by sixth century Gaelic customs Columcille's acts were strictly legal and were indeed his duty.

Just as journeys to Scotland and Ireland were necessary to understand the lands where he lived and worked, so it is necessary to journey back to the sixth century to study the society of his day.

His was a totally Celtic world and the key to much of what he thought and did is a Celtic key. The Celts, the basic blood stock of Europe, brought the Indo-European languages to the west. They were pioneers of metal work, whose iron swords gave them victory and whose iron tools cleared forests for cultivation. "The fine flower of the Iron Age" Dr. Nora Chadwick has called them. There can be few Europeans who are not enriched by much Celtic blood, yet most people know more about the ancient Egyptians or Greeks than they do about their gifted Celtic ancestors.

Did they originate beside the Caspian Sea or in the Danube valley? No one yet knows for sure. Nor what it was that pushed them forward on their great Folk Wanderings four thousand years ago. Nomadic herdsmen drifting west with their cattle, while warriors patrolled in war chariots and the women and children followed in carts. The Greeks called them *Keltoi* Celts. To the Romans they were *Galli*, the Gauls.

"The Danube is the land of the Celts and they are also beyond the Pillars of Hercules (Gibraltar)," recorded Herodotos about 450 BC by which date they were populating the British Isles. In the first century BC a man could travel from the Black Sea to the Atlantic and from Turkey to Scotland without leaving Celtic terrain.

Writings of their Roman foes depicted them as big blond fellows with fierce blue eyes and trailing moustaches, clad in tunic and trousers with wool cloaks of bright checks. They carried long iron swords, oval shields and thrusting spears. Most wore no helmet so that their elaborate coiffure could be admired. Strabo remarked, "Vanity makes them unbearable in victory and wholly downcast in defeat."

They looked on war as normal and desirable nor were they much concerned who they fought or why. Boasting and hard drinking were sufficient to cause a battle. As Polybius noted, "Their plans are dictated by the heat of their passions, not by cool calculation". Their leaders were war lords, fighting, feasting, plundering, headhunting and observing a savage code of honour. But for all their wide territories and high courage, the Celts never became a united political or military power. Like the Greeks, they had cultural unity in spite of political fragmentation.

Wave after wave of Celtic tribes arrived in Britain and Ireland during the 500 years before Christ, conquering and absorbing those who came before them. The Gaels, who were dominant in Ireland, spoke a Q-Celtic tongue, Gaelic. The Britons who populated the larger island, spoke a P-Celtic tongue, Welsh; that is, they tended to use a P sound where the Gaels used a Q or C sound. Thus "ceann", Gaelic for a head, became "pen" in Welsh.

British tribes extended as far north as the Firths of Clyde and Forth. Northwards lived the Cruithne in the land known as Alban. Their name is merely the Q-Celtic way of saying Prydyn or Briton and they were Celts in speech, beliefs and customs. But they did follow one unusual law. The sovereignty of their kings was inherited through the mother's line.

The Cruithne are better known as Picts, painted men, a nick-name given them by the Roman soldiers. The main body of the Pict nation lived north of the Firths but there were two separated groups, one in southwest Scotland and the other in County Down, Ireland. Columcille's foster father Cruithnechan was an Irish Cruithne and so were many of his closest friends. He spent so much of his life working among the Picts that they fill a large place in his story.

The last significant wave of Celts to arrive in Ireland came up the sealanes from Spain about 100 BC. Legend called them the Sons of Mil or Milesians and they were able to impose their overlordship upon the four earlier Irish kingdoms of Ulster, Connaught, Leinster and Munster. They carved for themselves a fifth kingdom of Meath, Ireland then presented a picture familiar in Europe of a warrior aristocracy ruling subject peoples of earlier immigrants.

These last invaders seem to have brought with them the

name Scoti referring perhaps to a family group. But it expanded until it was applied to all the Irish and for a thousand years Irishmen were known to neighbouring nations as Scoti.

"I have never been a day without slaying a Connaughtman and plundering by fire. I have always slept with the head of a Connaughtman under my knee."† So boasted the Ulster champion Conall-the-Victorious. The heroic sagas of the Ulster and the Fenian Cycles give a glimpse of ancient Ireland, full of treachery, violence and blood feuds, yet lit now and then by acts of sublime loyalty.

"They whole nation is war mad", wrote Strabo in the first century BC. "But otherwise they are not uncultivated." Pagan and fetich-ridden the Gaels certainly were, but not lacking in culture and law. Indeed every man's rank was defined by law, his honour price estimated and his rights and duties fixed.

Wealth was reckoned in cattle. A rich farmer rented his surplus cattle to poorer men, taking them under his protection. He himself was a client of a noble who was a client of a king, Ri. No man stood alone but was protected in his rights and bound by his duties. The greater a man's wealth the more his clients, the higher his rank and power. The client-protector relationship underpinned the whole society.

The Gael never thought of himself as a lone individual but always as part of his "true family", *derbfine*, which comprised all descendants of his great-grandfather. He spoke of his second cousins as brothers and sisters. The symbol of the *derbfine* was a hand, the palm being the great-grandfather, the first finger bones his sons, the second his grandsons and the third his great-grandsons. The *derbfine* symbol still appears on the flag of Ulster as the Red Hand.

The basic political unit was the *Tuath*, meaning a people, normally formed around a kinsman group, as loyalty to kinfolk was the most sacred social bond. They elected their own *Ri*. A number of *tuatha* would form a larger kingdom which itself would be part of one of the five over-kingdoms of Ulster, Connaught, Leinster, Munster and Meath. There were at least 150 kings of varying grades but the real power lay with the five over-Kings.

All kingship was both hereditary and elective; hereditary as to family, elective as to the individual. Men of the *derbfine* of the Royal Family were elighble for election. It was the privilege of the nobles to choose from among them the man they considered "most noble, experienced, wealthy, wise, learned, popular, free from blemish and best able to lead in battle." Such men were deemed king-worthy, *rigdomna*. Understandably Columcille all his life was regarded as *rigdomna*.

Primogeniture played no part in this system and it was rare for a son immediately to succeed his father. Usually the sceptre passed to a brother, nephew or cousin.

The king was a sacral figure, reincarnating the demi-god ancestor of his people, so fine looks and physique were important. His duties were to lead in war, to observe the sacred festivals and to uphold customary laws. Though he might act as arbiter, he was in no way a judge, lawgiver or governor.

Beside the king stood his adviser and chief judge. *Brieve.* He was a distinguished member of the order of *Filidh,* a special learned class. Youths from good families underwent a dozen years of rigorous training before graduating as *Filidh.* All instruction was oral and they sang their lessons, memorising the laws, histories and genealogies upon which every right of inheritance depended. There were ten grades of skill, rising to *Olave,* who was regarded as a great noble with a train of twenty-four attendants. However these were not servants but student *Filidh.* They were educated free of charge because the Gaels considered wisdom to be a common inheritance of the whole race, not a personal property.

Filidh were exempt from taxes and military service but debarred from holding land. Instead they enjoyed the right of *coinmed,* free food and lodging wherever they went. This special class were the judges, historians, poets, philosophers and physicians. They were also the priests for only they could conduct the sacrificial rites. In this role they were known as *Druid,* the ones who know.

The *Brieve* administered the Brehon laws, the oldest surviving legal code in Europe, which was based on assessing compensation for wrongs done. If a man was killed or wounded, the *Brieve* assessed the blood fine, *eric,* according to the amount of the victim's honour price.

The Gaels believed in reincarnation but the after life was not regarded as a reward for a virtuous life on earth nor were the Gods thought of as any more moral than mortals. The Other World was always close to them, nearer than foreign lands, and many hills were the dwellings of the *sidhe,* the fairies. Religion, central in every phase of life, was solely concerned with magic and mystic rites. Mortals walked in dread of offending any of the many capricious deities. Their conduct was ruled by strict observance of *gessa* and *buada,* taboos and good-luck.

Buada required, for instance, that a sacrificial victim, often human, be buried under the foundation of a new building. Mistletoe was *buada* and under the mistletoe bough a person could take liberties. Numbers, trees, animals and birds were known as lucky or unlucky. The salmon was lucky and sacred but the raven was deceitful and dangerous, while the crane was *gessa,* a bird of ill omen, and it was taboo to eat its flesh. The mere sight of three cranes flying overhead was enough to shake the morale of an army on the eve of battle.†

The Gaels armed themselves against the terrors of the unknown with charms and incantations and only the *Druid* knew the art of concocting them. Like all Celts they revelled in complicated rhymes, riddles and allusions. Hidden meanings and half-said things were always dearest to them.

These priestly poets were expected to be "the most just of men" and they often were. But greed corrupted some who lived like lazy parasites upon the working farmers, using satire and spells to terrorize their hosts and increase their own wealth and power. Superstition and hocus-posuc marked much of their ritual yet their seems to have been a sincere craving to breach the boundaries of the finite world so that the light of eternity might shine through. "A continual desire for union with the spirit," as W.B. Yeats put it, was at the root of the religion of the Gaels and may explain something of their swift response to Christianity.

"Who is God?" three daughters of the High King asked St. Patrick. "Where is His dwelling? Is He immortal? Is He in Heaven, or on earth, in the sea, in the rivers, the hills or the valleys? Has His Son been fostered by many? Is He found in youth or age? How is He discovered?" Perhaps these questions were in the hearts of many Gaels and the *Druid* strove to give them the answers. But they sought them vainly in occult arts and magic formulae.

The religious and political hierarchy of Ireland reached its summit in the person of the High King. *Ard Ri,* who reigned at Tara. He was the overload of all kings and only in his presence were the most sacred rites of the people celebrated. Twice, it is said, Columcille refused this exalted title and many of the most crucial events of his career focused at Tara. And so to examine the authority of the *Ard Ri,* let us follow the road to Tara of the Kings.

The god Nuadu-of-the-Silver-Hand: found near Armagh.

The hill of Tara is not much of a hill. It rises gently from the valley of the Boyne about 25 miles north-west of Dublin. The name means "place of view" and from the grassy ramparts of the old Royal Seat a surprisingly wide view stretches away in all directions. Perhaps this was why prehistoric dwellers chose the site for their passage tombs over 4000 years ago. Tara was already old as a sacred place when the Gaels adopted it as the seat of overlordship.

The origin of the High Kingship of Tara is lost in a fog of mystery but by the fourth century AD it had developed an aura as the pre-eminent dignity of all Ireland and the five over-Kings vied for the title of *Ard Rí.*

Theoretically the over-Kings elected to the office the most gifted man who was *rigdomna,* but in practice it fell as a prize to the prince who had the most clients and the sharpest weapons. The over-Kings rendered a somewhat reluctant homage to the *Ard Rí* as overlord but how much the title meant in actual fact depended on the toughness of the individual *Ard Rí* himself. Rebellion against him was never regarded as treason to Ireland.

In no way could the High King be compared to a Roman Caesar or a Norman feudal monarch. He reigned at Tara but he did not rule Ireland. Any attempt to do so would have met fierce opposition. His was an overlord-ship, reinforced by matrimonial alliances. He had no civil service through which to govern nor standing army to impose his will and for troops had to depend on those of his own dynastic kingdom. His ascendancy was chiefly supported by holding hostages from the subordinate kingdoms. Hostages ensured the payment of tribute. "A king without hostages is like a leaky keg of ale" said the Irish.

Nevertheless the *Ard Ri* was the supreme social and religious figure of Ireland. Only he could hold the *Feis* at Tara, the sacred rite by which the tribes of the Gaels "married" the land of Erin. Only he could convene the *Aenech* at Teltown every third year, the sacred assembly where the games were played and the laws reviewed by the *Brieves* and confirmed by the kings.

Splendour attended the inauguration of a new *Ard Ri* at the *Feis* of Tara. From all parts of Ireland came the voting Kings, their chariots following the five roads which converged on the enclosure at Tara where dwelt the *Ard Ri*. This was the setting for the *Banais-Ri*, the wedding of the new monarch to his realm.

No man, not even the king, dare utter a word until the Arch Druid had spoken. Glorious in his feathered cloak, he directed the ceremony of the Bull Feast. After a white bull had been sacrificed, the Arch Druid ate flesh and drank broth from it while around him the *Filidh* chanted "the song of truth" until he fell into a trance. In this state he "saw" who was the true heir and waking, proclaimed his name and titles. But if he lied his lips were doomed to wither.

No crown or throne figured in the rite. The *Ard Ri* was robed in white, a gold torque was placed around his neck and a purple cloak over his shoulders. Laying aside his sword, he took instead a white hazel sceptre, symbol of unsullied justice, and at the Stone of Destiny, *Lia Fail*, he pledged himself "to do right between man and man, whether weak or powerful."

Pagan and crude as much of the "wedding" symbolism was, nevertheless on that day the *Ard Ri* truly stood forth as the high priest, the reincarnated god-hero of his race.

The nuptial feast was held in the Mead Hall, 759 feet long by 46 wide which faced east and had seven doors. The shields of the nobles were hung on the walls in order of precedence and the guests filed to their seats. The *Ard Ri* sat at the north end between the queen and the Arch Druid and flanked by his guards. Silence fell when he struck a silver gong. Then he presented to the mightiest warrior present a roast boar, the Hero's Portion, *Curath Mir*. This called forth bardic songs of praise, drunken boastings and duels which often ended in bloodshed.

Prestige was of supreme importance to the *Ard Ri* since his real power depended on it. At all costs he must uphold his *enech*. Usually translated "honour," the word meant "face" in precisely the way the term is used in the Orient. Loss of face meant disaster. By stinginess, cowardice in battle or even using a hoe or plough a king could destroy his *enech*.

The *Filidh* wielded a deadly weapon against *enech*; the power of satire. Its devastating effect was illustrated in the famous saga *Tain Bo Cualinge* when used against a reluctant hero. "Queen Maeve sent the Druids to him that they might make three hurtful satires and three hilltop satires and raise three blisters on his face — shame, blemish and reproach — so that he might be dead before nine days."

The legendary *Ard Ri* Cormac macAirt of the third century AD, lost an eye in battle and felt the disfigurement so blemished his *enech* that he abdicated. Legend claimed he became a Christian during a long exile. His outline of the royal duties is instructive: "The king must have patience and self-government without haughtiness; speak the truth and keep promises; honour the nobles, respect the poets, adore God; keep the law exactly but with mercy; boundless in charity, care for the sick and orphans; lift up good men, suppress evil ones; freedom for the just, restriction for the unjust. At Samhain light the lamps and welcome the guests with clapping. Appear splendid as the sun in the Mead Hall at Tara."

Sometime around 400 AD Cormac's great-great-great grandson became *Ard Ri*, the ablest and most formidable ever to reign at Tara. Niall Noigiallach, Niall-of-the-Nine-Hostages, they called him and the praise ballads declared that he took hostages from the five Irish kingdoms and from the Britons, Picts, Gauls and Saxons as well. He certainly was a mighty slave raider. But his nine hostages more probably came from the small kingdom in the centre of Ulster, the Airgialla, meaning "those who gave hostages." He and his sons seemed to have smashed the power of the over-king of Ulster, taken two thirds of his territory and sacked his capital of Armagh.

Two of his sons, Eoghan and Conall Gulban, seized the western half of Ulster and ruled it from the mountain-top fortress of Grianan of Ailech overlooking Derry. Eoghan became king of Derry and Tyrone and Conall Gulban king of Donegal. Their two clans were known as the Northern Ui Neill.

Others of Niall's sons hacked out a kingdom for the Southern Ui Neill, mostly around Meath at the expense of the kingdom of Leinster. In sixty years fifteen pitched battles were fought. The enmity with Leinster was so bitter that when *Ard Ri* Laoghaire, chief of the Southern Ui Neill, died he was buried at Tara standing up in full armour, spear in hand, glowering south towards his Leinster foes.

Niall Noigiallach nursed the ambition that the High Kingship of Tara should belong to his family for ever and in fact the Ui Neill dynasty did hold it for 500 years.

Columcille was a prince of this fierce, warrior Royal Family, his great-grandfather being Conall Gulban, king of Donegal. All his life he walked with kings because they were his cousins.

This was his familiar world among the Gaelic-speaking Scoti who were his own folk. Warm-hearted but fickle, hospitable to a fault but remorseless in vengeance, swinging between extremes of joy and grief, "all their wars were merry and all their songs were sad". Great fighters and cattle thieves, great seamen and slave raiders, great singers to the harp and seers with "second sight". In his whole being Columcille was one of them, a Celt of the Celts and a Gael of the Gaels. Late in life he declared, "If death take me, I die for the love I bear the Gael. The Gael, the Gael-beloved name."

Irish warrior — Book of Kells.

St. Columba's lineage from the High Kings of Tara.

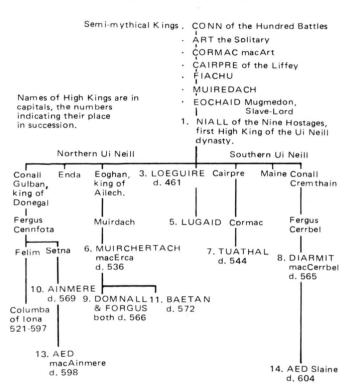

By inheritance he was heir to warrior kings but he was called Columcille, church dove, and he was profoundly a child of the Church. The drama of his life was the constant interaction of this double inheritance.

Christianity was still a novel belief of the Gaels, living on their island in the outer ocean far from the centre of the known world. It had taken root but Ireland was in no way yet a Christian country and the Church was still a pioneer community and its future remained precarious.

By what spiritual lineage had the faith of Jesus of Nazareth come to Columcille? No archaeological dig or yellowing parchment has yet revealed when Christianity first reached the British Isles but the historian of the Britons, St. Gildas, writing about 560 AD, said "Christianity came to Britain in the reign of Tiberius". That Emperor died in 37 AD only four years after the Crucifixion.

At first glance this seems incredible. But Phoenician ships regularly sailed from Tyre to Britain to load cargoes of Cornish tin. Tyre is a hundred miles from Jerusalem and sailors from the tin fleet may well have been in the crowd which heard St. Peter preach on that first Pentecost. From time immemorial the Patron Saint of the Cornish tin miners was Joseph of Arimathea, a village twelve miles from Tyre, and the old miners' song said "Joseph was in the tin trade."

By 210 AD Tertullian wrote of Britain "The Christians have reached regions inaccessible to Rome." In 240 Origen wrote "The Christian faith is a uniting force among the Britons," Three British bishops attended the Synod of

Arles in 314, so evidently the Gospel had taken firm root by the time that Constantine the Great brought toleration to the Church. But there is no sign that it had reached Ireland and it does not seem to have crossed the Irish Sea for another hundred years.

During the fourth century the Cross went forward but the Eagles of Rome fell back. Legions recruited from barbarians proved unstable, cheerfully hailing any politician as Caesar if the bribe was big enough. The Generals played lethal musical-chairs round the Imperial throne. The inevitable happened and the frontiers gave way. Gothic cavalry annihilated the legions at Adrianople and in 410 the Goths sacked Rome itself.

Something of the shock of that incredible event lingers in the words of St. Jerome. "O weep for the Empire! Mainz razed, Lyons devastated. I can't mention Toulouse without tears. Suddenly comes news of Rome's fall. The light of all the earth is extinguished."

In the darkness of collapse one beacon fire burnt bright. It had been lit by an officer of the elite Imperial Cavalry Guard whose name was Martin. He read *The Life of St. Anthony* by Athanasias and the book changed his life. It fired his imagination for the monastic ideal. Later when he was elected Bishop of Tours in Gaul he founded the Magis Monasterium in 371 where he trained his monks, not as contemplative hermits, but as a disciplined Christian colony. An extreme of evil can only be countered by an extreme of good and Martin's standards of poverty, chastity and obedience were a direct challenge to the plunder, debauch and anarchy which were the norm in most of Europe.

"Monastic life was not a selfish quest for personal purity", wrote Geoffrey Ashe. "Monks built a new society in the shell of the old. Here social distinctions were effaced, fresh scope was given to ability. Their community witnessed to the world's corruption... The monks built well enough to save Europe from total ruin."†

Young men, nobles and nobodies, poured in to Tours to be trained by this soldierly man who was "never angry, worried, sad, frivolous or gloomy-faced." And from the trianing camp went out men acting from a new motive, "for love of God". They owned nothing, they coveted nothing and they feared nothing. The uncouth invaders were baffled by them, awed and won.

Among the young who came to learn from Martin was a Briton named Ninian, on his way home after studying in Rome. When he finally left he took some Gallic stonemasons with him to help build a worthy church, because the art of stonemasonry was not yet understood in his area. He was born, it is said, on the Solway Firth not far from the west end of Hadrian's Wall in the kingdom of the Britons of Strathclyde. The site he chose for his new church was further west along the Firth among the Picts of Galloway, where the southwest corner of Scotland points across the sea to Ireland.

While building the church in 397 Ninian heard of the death of St. Martin and named the new monastery after him. But the local folk called it "Candida Casa," the white house, now Whithorn, because of the gleaming white plaster the Gallic mason used on its walls. Parts of the plastered walls can still be seen.

Ninian's mission seems to have taken him chiefly

among the Britons of Strathclyde and the Picts of Galloway, though church dedications to his name occur on the
Moray Firth and further north. Some writers claim that he
was the first to bring Christianity to what is now Scotland.
However probably his own people, the Britons of Strathclyde, were already Christians. But this is certain. Had it
not been for the men and women he trained at Candida
Casa, Christianity might well have disappeared from Britain along with Rome's legions.

On the shore near Whithorn is the Physgyll Cave where
Ninian used to withdraw to pray. How often, looking
across to Ireland, he must have wondered who God would
send with the Gospel to win the Scoti. There is a tradition
he went himself to work in Leinster.

Irish slave-raiders were on the loose in the early 400s and
rounded up thousands of captives in Britain, like 16-year-
old Succath, better known to history as St. Patrick. He was
sold in Ulster and set to work as a shepherd. On the lonely
hills of Slemish he found faith in God, then when he was
22 he managed to escape and make his way home. In his
mind burnt a determination to win the Irish for Christ.

Almost all that is known about St. Patrick is in his
Confession, written late in life; and in his wrathful *Letter
to Coroticus*, King Ceredic of Strathclyde, whose soldiers
had sold Christian captives to the Picts. "A wicked rebel
against Christ, no longer fit to be a fellow citizen of devout
Romans!" stormed Patrick, demanding that he rescue
these slaves.

St. Patrick, who left such a sublime mark on Ireland,
left hardly a trace in the records. When and where he was
born, who trained and ordained him, when he came to

Ireland and when he died are all unknown. Was there one
Patrick or two? Was he a Gaul or a Briton? Did he die in
461 or in 496? No wonder the fifth century is called the
"lost century"!

Yet St. Patrick was no myth. His coming to Ireland was
the most important event in Irish history. His life, which
has so tantalised historians, cannot be debated here.
Instead we must ask why his mission succeeded so powerfully. In many of the traditions and legends there recurs
the theme of forgiveness. It may be a clue.

It is said that the *Ard Ri* invited St. Patrick to join a
committee of learned *Brieves* to purify and write down the
Brehon Laws, formerly transmitted orally. In the introduction of the resulting Great Record, *Senchus Mor*, it is
written "Retaliation prevailed in Ireland before Patrick;
and Patrick brought forgiveness with him. So now no one
is put to death for his crimes so long as the blood-fine, *eric*,
is paid."

He himself had been kidnapped, enslaved and exploited. By every law known to the Irish, he had a right to seek
vengeance. Instead he came back to them with the gift of
forgiveness. Could warm-hearted Gaels resist that? "Forgive us our sins as we forgive those who sin against us."
Patrick was a living embodiment of Christ's words.

But consider the implications of forgiveness in a society
structured around the blood-feud. Much of the creative
passion of the people was locked up in the sterile, unend-
ing tit-for-tat of revenge. Patrick broke the cycle and freed
the Gaels for greatness. His dates may be obscure but what
he did for the Irish is written large on their subsequent
history.

The Church which Patrick founded was on a tribal basis. As there were no cities, the *tuath* was the only social framework able to sustain it. Angus the Culdee wrote of Patrick's clergy, "They were all bishops, famous and holy founders of churches, 350 in number." A large force of bishops was not unique to Ireland. At this period there were 400 bishops in Asia Minor who were termed "Chorespiscop" — country bishops — and it required only one bishop to consecrate them. They were not diocesan and had no administrative duties as the Church was still in a missionary phase. In Germany about 700 AD St. Willibrod used the same system.

Towards the end of Patrick's life collegiate groups of bishops were formed, seven brothers of one family, meaning probably the Celtic corporate family, *derbfine*. The Church was secular, the clergy living wholly integrated with the *tuath* they served.

Most occupations among the Gaels were hereditary, so as the first generation of converts passed away it was perfectly natural for the grade of Bishop to become hereditary. Nor did the heirs cease to be Christian, but their prime loyalty was the *tuath* and in any conflict they tended to be more clansmen than priests.

St. Patrick was not alone in the work of converting Ireland. A sustained effort came from Wales, affecting the kingdoms of Leinster and Munster, and indeed in the earliest documents there is hardly a mention of Patrick. How then did he become the pre-eminent figure, the Patron Saint of Ireland?

Perhaps it was because of his influence upon the sons of Niall-of-the-Nine-Hostages, several of whom he baptised.

His work was predominantly in the north and he made
many converts among the royal families of Ulster and
Connaught. As the illustrious dynasty of the Ui Neill rose
to power at Tara it was natural that they should give pride
of place to their ancestral "father in God" and to his
episcopal church at Armagh.

Martin — Ninian — Patrick, who baptised king Conall
Gulban of Donegal. That was the spiritual lineage of
Columcille. This brief outline of his background may
give something of a setting for his life as we resume the
story.

*Latinus stone at Whithorn — oldest Christian monument in
Scotland, c. 450 A.D.*

Ireland during the decade in which Columcille came to manhood seems to have been fairly peaceful. When he was 15 or so his cousin the High King Murcertach macErca died. Although he was recorded as the first Christian to reign at Tara, the myths woven round his death were as weirdly magical as anything in the Dark Ages. He was succeeded by Tuathal Maelgarb who was one of the Southern Ui Neill and inclined towards the Druid's teaching.

The young prince must have pondered deeply over the choice which would decide the whole course of his life but no tradition indicates a crisis of decision in Columcille's early years. His boyhood habit of prayer, which earned him a nickname, appears to deepen steadily into a commitment.

At Moville under his tutor Bishop Finbar he received a thorough grounding in Latin by means of memorizing the Psalms. In monastic life the Psalms played an enormous part, since there was as yet little other sacred music. They were recited in private devotions, sung at every church service, the monks marched out to work and rowed their boats to their cadence. They were chanted at happy times and as penance and the dead were laid to rest to their music.

The student moved on to learn the classics, literature, philosophy and some science. Bishop Finbar was a wise teacher, a widely travelled man who had crossed the sea to get his Church training at Candida Casa where since the days of St. Ninian Christian youths had been educated in a mainly Roman scholarship.

At Moville Columcille met for the first time something of the scope and breadth of foreign culture from Rome and it stimulated his questing mind. He developed an urge to explore the root causes of things, whether they were the cycles of the tides, the habits of fish or the behaviour of people. And it was during this time that he chose the ideals for his own life. He asked God for the gift of purity; the gift of wisdom; and the gift of prophecy. Aims for the body, mind and soul. At the end of his training with Bishop Finbar he was ordained deacon.

He next moved down to Leinster, the land of his mother's origin, to be tutored by Gemmen, a Christian who was a learned member of the *Filidh*, With him he studied the Celtic wisdom of his own cultural heritage. He mastered the intricate rules of poetry and rhetoric, the lore of Nature and the rudiments of medicine. He learnt the Brehon Laws of his people, essential knowledge for a prince of the dynasty. Thus his education bridged the oral wisdom of the Celtic past and the written scholarship of Rome.

While he was with Gemmen Columcille faced the first great crisis of his life. One day tutor and pupil were studying in the open air when a girl raced towards them calling for help. Her pursuer stabbed her to death, his spear passing through the very cloak of the young deacon who had tried to shield her. Columcille cursed the murderer. "Whereupon" reported Adomman in his book, "he fell dead as did Ananias at the feet of St. Peter."

If Columcille's curse had the power to slay, it seems curious that he did not curse the man before he killed the girl. But perhaps there is a hint in the words" . . . as did Ananias."

Battlefield of Culdremne beneath Ben Bulben on Sligo Bay. Shrine of the Cathach treasured for centuries by O'Donnells of Donegal.

Road to the Isles
*PRO CHRISTO PEREGRIN ARI VOLENS — pilgrimage for the
love of Christ.*

Adomnan's object was to show the saint exercising the same power as the Apostle. Maybe the murderer went jeering on his way only to fall foul of the girl's avenging kinsmen. Whatever happened, great awe fell on the country folk that the doom of Columcille's curse had so swiftly overtaken the killer. It would be wrong to imply that Adomnan doctored the story. He probably wrote it just as it was told to him. To the local people the point was that Columcille cursed the murderer and he died, when and how being in their view minor details.

Such random violence was common an Irish society and, though deplored, it was accepted as inevitable much as death on the highway is accepted today. But the impact of this tragedy on Columcille was abiding and he refused passively to tolerate this evil. He became convinced that the innocent, defenceless and fugitive must be protected from vengeance and that the Church must establish inviolable sanctuary for them. On this principle he never wavered.

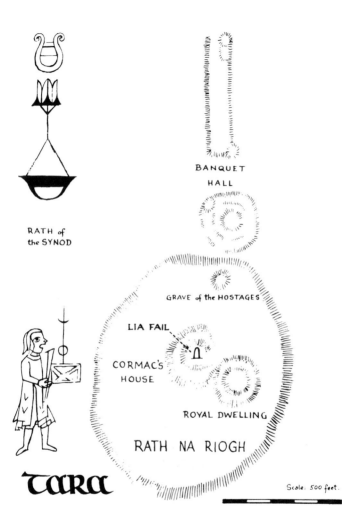

RATH of
the SYNOD

BANQUET
HALL

GRAVE of the HOSTAGES

LIA FAIL

CORMAC'S
HOUSE

ROYAL DWELLING

RATH NA RIOGH

TARA

Scale. 500 feet.

At Clonard twenty miles west of Tara there grew up the most influential seat of learning in Ireland. Today the River Boyne meanders through the water meadows of Clonard beside a dome-shaped hill fifty feet high, crowned by a noble chestnut tree. But in the 540s AD around this landmark were gathered the huts of three thousand students.

The founder of Clonard was Finian, a Cruithne who as a youth had crossed over to Wales to learn monastic discipline from the Welsh saints Cadoc, David and Gildas. He longed to go on to Rome to extend his education but was halted by a vivid dream. A voice told him, "All you would find in Rome will be given to you here. Go and renew faith in Ireland after Patrick." He obeyed and Clonard was the result.†

"They came from every point to learn wisdom... from the tutor of the saints, a doctor of wisdom like unto St. Paul, who sent out rays of teaching." They came from every background. Brendan from Trales was a sailor, an older monk. Kenneth (Cainnech) was a Cruithne, son of a bard. Ciaran mac-an-tsaor was a carpenter's son from a pre-Celtic subject tribe, who arrived driving a dun cow to provide his needs. Mobhi had been hideously disfigured in an accident and was nicknamed Clairenach, flat face. The Gaels had a horror of physical deformity yet Mobhi was welcomed as a student as warmly as the handsome prince-deacon, Columcille.

Each was allotted a place near the chapel to build his hut of wattle and thatch and each was expected to grind his daily ration of corn in a quern. Columcille completed this chore faster than anyone, to the annoyance of slower comrades. And the banks of the Boyne were their lecture halls.

Clonard attracted these young men because Finnian dealt with the fundamental issue of the meaning of Man's existence. The Druids too had sought the answer, hoping to find the link between the mortal and the spirit world. They had delved in magic but only mystified themselves with their own mysteries.

The link, Finnian taught, was God. Not a remote Eochaid-the-Horseman-of-Heaven or Lugh-of-the-Long-Arm, but a Voice speaking in the intimacy of the heart. As St. Cadoc put it "Conscience is the eye of God in a man's soul."†

"God loves me" — the greatest fact of all time. On discovering this, a man longed to live every hour in the presence of that Love. The purpose of existence was to live so as to enter eternal life. Herein lay the dynamic and magnetism of the monastic way.

The world around was dominated by the economics of plunder, with massacre, slavery, famine and plague trotting behind like jackals. These evils happened because men refused to seek first the Kingdom of God and therefore the monks focused their hearts, minds and wills wholly on God.

The means: to love Him and love His children. "Love is Heaven, hate is Hell" in Cadoc's phrase. The monastic rule helped them to do this systematically so as to reproduce in themselves the likeness of Christ. The monks' total concentration on God was divine logic which to the worldly seemed foolish.

The training of the students was based on memorising the Word of God, just as the Filidh memorised the words of the ancients. They worked in teams of three to keep continual prayer and psalms being offered in the chapel and took turns to conduct worship.

Finnian's method was clinical. "By contraries let us cure contraries", he taught. "Practise patience to cure anger; kindness for envy; tongue-discipline for slander; joy for depression; generosity for greed." He taught them to use confession: "Evil thoughts shrivel when made public." The value of fasting; "Moses fasting talked with God." And the importance of manual work: "A monk who works is plagued by one devil, an idle monk by a thousand."

He showed them how "as spiritual doctors to treat with diverse cures the sins of gluttony, fornication, avarice, anger, dejection, languor and pride." Each helped the other as an *amn chara*, soul friend: "A man without an *amn chara* is like a body with no head." And they learnt from each other, humility from one, silence or gentleness from another. They often made the sign of the Cross: "Where the Cross passes evil is powerless."

They took their own medicine. Ciaran the carpenter's son was jealous of the popular Columcille. In a dream Ciaran saw laid before him an axe, a plane and an auger, and heard the words, "These carpentry tools are all you have sacrificed to God. But Columcille has sacrificed the sceptre of Ireland." Envy died and a close friendship took its place.

Ninnidh "Squint-eye" was too poor to buy a book and appealed to Finnian who gave him permission to borrow one, if he could. But Books were few and precious and lending a book might halt a student's own studies. Nobody would loan him one and he returned to Finnian in despair. "Go to the boy across the green," said the teacher. "This was Ciaran who owned one book, St. Matthew's Gospel and he was halfway through learning it. He had just read, "Whatsoever you would that men should do to you, so do to them." At that moment Ninnidh arrived asking to borrow the book and Ciaran handed it over.

Later when the story got around, some of the students teased Ciaran, calling him "half-Matthew". But Finnian said, "No, call him half-Ireland because half Ireland will follow his example."

An important part of each day's work was copying the Bible and other sacred texts such as the Life of St. Anthony by Athanasius, the Confessions and the City of God by Augustine and the Life of St. Martin by Sulpicius Severus. Perhaps no generation has known the Bible more thoroughly. They accepted it as the guide book of life, believing that what happened in the first century would happen in the sixth. They expected miracles and they were not disappointed.

The challenge at Clonard was heroic, leaving no room for the mediocre. But these high-spirited Irishmen had been weaned on stories of Finn macCunaill and the Fianna, elite troops who underwent rugged testing before being initiated into the corps. Like a new Fianna, they responded to any discipline or sacrifice necessary to fit them to be "Milites Christi."

They dared to dream of establishing on earth colonies of the Kingdom of Heaven, places where men would live under the direction of God's love as fully as in Eternity. In these colonies they would be free — free from the greed of possessions, the hates and fears of ambition, the cruelties of pride, and where in serving others they would find freedom from self. In simple honesty they accepted the most revolutionary aim ever put into human words, "They Will be done on earth as it is in Heaven."

"You chosen generation", they read in Augustine's Confession, "You weak things of the world, who have forsaken all to follow the Lord, go after Him, confound the mighty. Go after Him, shine in all the world, you beautiful fires, run to and fro, be known in all nations." What music to pluck the harp strings of Gaelic souls!

Initial letter (enlarged), penned by Columcille; in the Cathach.

Chapter eight

The audacity of these young Clonard militants was startling and the impact of these literate, articulate, enthusiastic monks on Irish society may well be imagined. They were unprecedented and unpredictable; small wonder that some of the hereditary clergy viewed them with alarm.

What was so revolutionary was that they had passed beyond the confines of tribalism, in an age when tribal loyalty was regarded as the highest social virtue. Though drawn from all classes of the five kingdoms, the monks shared a common vision, a discipline and a higher loyalty which overtopped clan or caste barriers. They were a professional army of Christian educators and as such were a threat to the established ways of both the Druids and the stand-pat churchmen.

As the monks fanned out across the land, "little Clonards" sprang up until all Ireland "was glittering with saints as numerous as the stars." In that age the term saint meant a man committed to live a Christian life, not one canonised by the Church.

There is a tale that Finnian wished Columcille to become a bishop, but when he went to be consecrated he found the Bishop ploughing and, scorning to receive Holy Orders from a ploughman, came away and remained thereafter just a priest.

The story does not hold together very well, Columcille, who had refused a sceptre and regularly did the slave's chores of querning corn and washing travellers' feet, would scarcely scorn a ploughman. Anyway the

ploughman-bishop was Etchan, brother of king Aed of
Ailech and Columcille's own cousin. The tale seems to be
a later invention to explain why so great a saint was only a
priest. The real truth behind the matter will be discussed
in a later chapter.

Twelve of the Clonard priests trained by Finnian gave
such leadership and left such a mark on their age that they
became known as the Twelve Apostles of Ireland.

There were:

> Ciaran who founded Saighir monastery in Munster.
> Ciaran mac-an-tsaor who founded Clonmacnois on
> the Shannon.
> Colman macCrimthan of Terryglass.
> Mobhi Clairenach of Glasnevin.
> Ninnidh of Inismacsaint.
> Brendan of Birr.
> Brendan the Sailor of Clonfert.
> Laisren of Devenish.
> Ruadhan of Lothra.
> Sennell of Cloninnis.
> Kenneth (Cairnnech) of Achabo.
> Columcille of Iona.

Although princely rank and dynamic personality
tended to make Columcille "first among equals", when
the young monks left Clonard he refused to be the leader.
He, Kenneth and fifty others went to Glasnevin, near
Dublin, where they placed themselves under Mobhi Flat-
face as their Abbot. We catch a glimpse of the athletic and
impetuous young Columcille. On a stormy night he was
returning to his monastery through the downpour when
he found his way barred by the River Tolka in rain-

swollen spate. He plunged in and swam across the torrent rather than be late for Vespers.

It was here that Columcille became friends with Comgall, an Ulster warrior turned priest, who was to found the famous missionary college at Bangor. At this time the carpenter's son Ciaran mac-an-tsaor was founding Clonmacnois abbey on the banks of the river Shannon, destined to become one of Europe's eminent seats of learning.

Far away at Pelusium in Egypt about 540 AD plague broke out. It was bubonic or Yellow Plague and within two years it reached Constantinople, making its first appearance in Europe. For four months it killed up to 10,000 people a day in over-crowded Constantinople. Then the infection, carried by fleas, "spread over the entire world afflicting all without mercy", in the words of Procopius. The noted bacteriologist Dr. Hans Zinsser called it, "a calamity rarely equalled in history. The greatest of all pandemics that helped to undermine the ancient civilization."† Towns were left without people, freeman and serf alike fled from the farms and harvests lay on the ground rotting.

The plague reached Britain and Ireland about 548 AD, spreading inland from the ports. Ciaran the carpenter's son, still in his early thirties, died of it and so did Colman at Terryglass. It took the life of the valiant teacher of Clonard, St. Finnian, but he had completed his work of "renewing the faith in Ireland after Patrick."

Abbot Mobhi ordered all his monks to disperse from Glasnevin in the hope that some would survive. Kenneth crossed over to Wales to work with St. Cadoc. Columcille went home to Donegal where his cousin king Aed of

Ailech offered him an old fort in the oak forest of Derry as
a site for a monastery.

The location delighted him from the first moment he
saw it, the great oaks growing beside the tidal waters of
Lough Foyle. But he felt he must refuse the gift because he
was still a monk under the authority of Abbot Mobhi.
Then messengers arrived with the news that Mobhi Flat-
face had died of the plague and sent Columcille his
Abbot's girdle with his dying wish that he should found a
new monastery.

He built his first chapel among the oaks he so loved. It
was the universal practice to site churches on an east-to-
west axis. But Columcille found that to do so here would
necessitate cutting down a majestic oak. He built the
chapel on a north-to-south axis instead. So Derry came
into existence, called in Gaelic *Doirecholmcille* —
Columcille's Oak.

> "But Sweeter and fairer to me
> The salt sea where the gulls cry
> When I come to Derry from afar —
> Sweeter to me."

Chapter nine

In the age of motor travel the sea is a barrier but it was different in the fourth century when most travel and trade moved by boat. Then Britain and Ireland were united, rather than divided, by the Irish Sea. From Brittany to the Hebrides was one long, watery "Main Street" and up and down it sailed the trading ships, with tin from Cornwall, wheat from Anglesey, wine from Britanny and wolf hounds from Ireland. The Gaels were great seamen and ranged as far as the Faroes and Iceland to bring back eiderdown feathers and peregrine falcons.

The work-a-day freight ship was the curragh, a wooden frame covered by greased hide making it tough but light. Galway fishermen still use them. It was cheap to build, light to handle and practical for working in surf off an open beach. In Columcille's day Ireland was linked with the other Celtic lands by an ever-moving bridge of trading curraghs. Events on one side of the Irish Sea directly affected the other side.

What had been happening in Britain since the days of St. Ninian? After three centuries Rome's legions had gone. But it did not happen suddenly and the Britons went on thinking of themselves as Romans. They had the difficult job of taking over their own administration and of improvising an army with very few trained people, because it had been forbidden by Roman law for Britons to bear arms or have military training.

The threat to Britain was still the Picts from the north. Hadrian's Wall, built in 122 AD from sea to sea between Newcastle and Carlisle, and the Antonine turf wall between the Forth and the Clyde, had checked this menace for many years. But in Rome's grand strategy Britain had always been expendable and the Wall's garrisons were constantly weakened to aid other fronts. So long as the enemy's attacks were haphazard it was a reasonable risk.

But in 367 AD the unthinkable happened. Pricts, Scoti and Saxons all attacked at once and the defences were swamped. For a year the raiders pillaged at will until Theodosius brought over an army and chased them out.

Reading the records of the years after the Great Raid it is clear that someone was trying to prepare the Britons to defend themselves. That man may have been Magnus Clemens Maximus commanding the army in Britain.

Between the two Walls lived two powerful pro-Roman tribes, the Votadini in the east, the Dumnonii in the west. About 370 AD five thousand of their men were enrolled as feoderati, auxiliary troops, and formed into three infantry and six cavalry regiments named Britanniciani Juniores. The Votadini regiments under the command of Cunedda, a Roman-Briton, marched from Hadrian's Wall to north Wales to drive out the Scoti invaders who were settling down to stay. The Irish Scoti from Laigin (Leinster) were so firmly entrenched that their name still remains on the Lleyn peninsula in Wales. Around 390 Cunedda drove them out and from his descendants came the dynasty of the kingdom of Gwynedd in North Wales.

Magnus Maximus himself was a Spaniard but he married a Briton, Helena, daughter of King Eudav of Dumnonia. Their descendants appear to have become one of the royal lines of Strathclyde. According to the Gaulish

Chronicle "Maximus strenuously overcame the Picts and the Scots."

But in the Empire things were going disastrously wrong. The Goths had smashed through the Danube frontier and their cavalry was threatening to cut Britain off from Rome. In 383 the legion at York hailed Magnus Maximus as Emperor, and having done what he could for the Britons, he took his troops over the Channel to save Gaul. He was acknowledged as Augustus (deputy Emperor) for five years, then defeated and killed by Theodosius.

But he left a warm memory with the Britons, and the ancient Welsh book Mabinogion said, "Macsen Wledig was emperor, the best fitted of all who went before him."

By 410 the legions had gone for ever and the Britons were on their own. To make things worse they were deeply divided by the heresy of Pelagius. He was a Briton who claimed that men could obtain perfection by their own unaided effort and had no need of foregiveness or the grace of God. It was a popular doctrine with the comfortable and self-satisfied and Bede described the Pelagians as "resplendent in attire and surrounded by adulation."† Politically they tended to be opposed to Rome and they put their support behind the government of a leader called Vortigern.

The orthodox clergy, in distress over the growing schism, wrote for help to Gaul and the Bishops there recommended that the Pope send men to counter the heresy. Pope Celestine commissioned Bishop Germanus of Auxerre and Bishop Lupus of Troyes.

Germanus was a remarkable Roman-Gaul who had been Governor of the Province of Amorica when the populace had elected him as their Bishop. Much against his will he accepted but then gave himself wholly to the work of the Church.

Germanus and Lupus crossed from Britanny in 429 to Plymouth Sound and made their way to St. Albans, site of Britain's first martyrdom. At this sacred place they called a Synod of all Church leaders and in public debate routed the Pelagians.

Nennius, the ninth century scribe, stated that Germanus ex-communicated Vortigern who promptly sent for twelve Druids to be his advisers. From that time on there seem to have been two parties among the Britons: the Druidic "Native Party" and the Christian "Roman Party".

Marauding bands of Picts, combined with Saxons who had based in the Orkneys since the Great Raid, were terrorising the midlands of Britain. Germanus had been a soldier and he retrained the dispirited regiments of Britanniciani during the winter. By spring, with discipline and morale high, they were fit for battle. Germanus enticed the raiders to attack his army up a steep valley in the Welsh mountains near Mold. He had troops in ambush on both flanks and as the enemy charged up the valley he gave the signal. The whole British army sprang up shouting "Alleluia!" Echoes in the hills added confusion to surprise and the enemy panicked and fled, many drowning in the rain-swollen river Alyn as they tried to escape from the valley. The Alleluia victory won a respite of a dozen years.

Plague, perhaps scarlet fever, struck in 444 AD. Said

Bede, "A terrible plague fell on Britain destroying so many that the living scarce sufficed to bury the dead. They consulted how to obtain help to repel the attacks of their fierce northern neighbours, and all agreed with Vortigern to call in the Saxons." It was an old Roman policy to hire Germans as border guards.

Vortigern hired three shiploads of exiled Saxons led by their chief Hengist. His son Octa took the mercenaries to the north, drove the Picts back beyond the Roman Walls, then settled beside the river Tweed, claiming it as their "sword room". From this germ grew the mighty Anglo-Saxon kingdom of Northumbria.

At this precise time, 450 AD, Europe was convulsed. Out of Asia came Attila and his Huns, hideous, sub-human horsemen who swept across Germany and Gaul. Terrified Saxons and Frisians fled across the North Sea. They came as refugees and many returned to Germany when the Hun scare was over. But to the Britons it was like an invasion and they resisted.

A cavalry officer from Britanny called Illtud came over as a volunteer to help the Britons fight the invading hea-then Saxons but what he saw of the behaviour of the Christian soldiers made him decide that spiritual recovery had to precede military recovery. He became a monk and his training school at Llanilltud in south Wales produced great leaders such as St. Samson of Britanny, St. David of Wales, St. Cadoc and St. Gildas. Samson said, "Of all Britons Illtud was the most accomplished in the Scrip-tures and in every kind of learning, geometry, grammar, arithmetic." He was the first Abbot to add intellectual studies to the training of monks. His pupils Cadoc and

Gildas educated St. Finnian and sent him back to Ireland
to do his mighty work at Clonard.

*Magnus Maximus, Augustus of the West, 383 A.D. From a coin
minted at Trier, now in the British Museum.*

Chapter ten

Prosperous peace came to Britain in the last twenty years of the fifth century under the leadership of Ambrosius Aurelianus, head of the Roman Party, who checked the Saxon inroads. Britain was now bisected north to south by a borderland stretching from the Edinburgh area down to Southampton. It was not a fixed line but an intermix of pockets of Britons and Saxons but the Saxons dominated the east coast.

Britannia of the Britons still comprised the larger western half of the island and there the political power appeared to have crystallized around the military organizations left by the Romans. By far the strongest British kingdom was the Dumnonii of Strathclyde, whose territory stretched from Loch Lomond down to the river Ribble in Lancashire. Its capital was at Dumbarton (Fort of the Britons) on the Clyde with a subordinate kingdom of Cumbria which had its capital at Carlisle. Both towns were at the western terminals of the two Roman Walls.

The Roman party was strong at Strathclyde. For three hundred years Roman soldiers had taken their discharge, married and settled in this area and though their children spoke the mothers' tongue, they thought of themselves as Romans. Here too were based the Dumnonian cohorts of the Britanniciani Juniores and for centuries to come the men of the North were to boast the title of "Britons of the Green Standard", recalling the green dragon standards of these cohorts.

The Dumnonii of Strathclyde were kinsmen of the Dumnonii who lived in Somerset, Devon and Cornwall, with their capital at Exeter. Both spoke the same Cornish-type P-Celtic and their royal houses were closely related. They were not too tribes with similar names but were, it seems, two branches of one people.

The other strong British kingdom was Gwynedd in north Wales. Cunedda's descendants and his Votadini regiments had established themselves in the corn-growing island of Anglesey and their power extended along the Welsh coast between the old Roman bastions of Chester and Caernarvon. The kings of Gwynedd bore the title of Island Dragon, a reference to the red standard of their cohorts. From this evolved *Y Ddraig Goch* — the Red Dragon of Wales.

The Saxon Revolt, as St. Gildas has called it, exploded about the beginning of the sixth century. The term revolt indicates an uprising of inhabitants, not an overseas invasion. The Anglo-Saxons who had been established for two generations in Berwickshire and the Lothians attacked along the south bank of the Forth towards Stirling, into the land known to the Britons as Gododdin. They were led by Ossa, descended from Hengist.

Meanwhile in the south a Saxon with a Celtic name, Cerdic, landed at Southampton about 500 AD and began to carve out a kingdom for the West Saxons. Far away up north in Argyll at this very time Fergus and Lorn macErc were planting their colony of Dalriad Scots.

A champion to match the crisis arose among the Britons. Arthur, nicknamed "the Bear", was the successor to Ambrosius as leader of the Roman Party. He was not a king despite the legends, but his title was Dux Bellorum, Battle Commander. Probably he was Dumnonian, but

whether of south or north may have been unimportant.
The Britons thought of their land as one battleline as is
shown by the word Deheubarth, meaning "right flank",
which was applied to the south Wales area and the words
Gwyr Y Gogledd, meaning "men of the North" and applied to the Strathclyde forces.† Arthur's command
embraced the whole of Britannia. Myths have almost obli-
terated his historical outline but this much is certain. He
stirred the imagination of the Britons as no one before or
since.

He defeated the Saxons and their Pict allies in twelve
battles and his chief opponent appears to have been Ossa.
His victories were won, some think, by the daring handling of cavalry, using stirrups and charging home, lance
in rest, to strike with the whole weight of the horse and
man. This was still a relatively new method of horse
fighting learnt from the Goths, and the Saxons had not
developed a cavalry force to counter it.

The last and decisive battle was about 516 AD at Mount
Badon, thought to be Liddington Castle near Swindon.
Archaeology has found evidence that there was a major
Saxon retreat early in the 500s after a disaster somewhere
between Reading and Gloucester.

Mount Badon halted Saxon expansion for half a century. It enabled the Britons to enjoy twenty years of peace
behind a frontier guarded by a chain of garrisoned towns
established by Arthur.

"As those who had lived through the Saxon Revolt
gradually died off", wrote St. Gildas in his history *The
Destruction of Britain*, "there succeeded a generation who
were ignorant of that storm and accustomed only to enjoy-

ing the present peace. The controlling influences of truth and justice were shattered, bringing total dissolution to church and state. The very memory of virtues disappeared."

The dream of Arthur's life and his whole aim was to unite the Christian princes of Britain and drive out the pagan invaders. Militarily he had succeeded brilliantly and given his people victory. But he could not get the Britons to unite: victory had not brought truth and justice. The tragedy of Arthur was that the peace he had won was broken in the end, not by the Saxons, but by civil war among the Britons.

Arthur had entrusted Dunpelder, a defensive town in Gododdin near Edinburgh, to the command of King Loth, from whom the Lothians take their name. He was described as "rex semipaganus."

About 537 AD Loth's son Mordred headed an insurrection of Native Party Britons and Pict freebooters. Arthur and his troops faced them at Camlann and in battle both Arthur and Mordred were killed.†

Arthur's death was a disaster for the Roman Party and a triumph for the pagan Native Party, who pushed their advantage, driving out the Christians wherever they had the power. Throughout the North churches flamed and the faithful fled or died. *The Annales Cambriae* compiled in the ninth century give this record for the year 537 AD —"Arthur and Mordred fell at Camlann: and many died in Britain and Ireland."

This was no local quarrel but a civil war affecting not only Britain but Ireland too. A great war of faiths.

Chapter eleven

Into the story now comes a man who was destined to be Columcille's inspiring fellow-worker in the years of danger and struggle which were beginning. He was a Strathclyde Briton named Kentigern, though to the Scots he was usually known as St. Mungo (*Mwyn-cu-* beloved one). Legends befog his birth but it is probable that his mother was Tannoch, daughter of King Loth of Dunpelder, the "rex semi-paganus". Because she became a Christian, her father persecuted her and, although she was pregnant, set her adrift in an open boat upon the Firth of Forth. Wind and tide carried her ashore at Culross and there her son was born about 518 AD. He was brought up by the village priest and on reaching manhood was himself ordained.

After the death of Arthur the Roman Party of Strathclyde had rallied behind the leadership of the young King Rhydderch Hael — the Generous. In 543 he invited Kentigern, who was only twenty-five, to become bishop of a Christian settlement at Cathures, now Glasgow, where a church founded by St. Ninian still served a persecuted few.

But the pagan tide was in full spate. In Gododdin priests died as martyrs, among them Derad, son of the saintly King Brychan. In a couple of years Morken and the Druid faction drove Rhydderch Hael from his throne and he sought refuge with his mother's people in Ireland. Next year Bishop Kentigern had to flee for his life. The historian St. Gildas, son of a minor king, was also driven out.

In exile Gildas wrote his history *De Excidio Britanniae* — "The Destruction of Britain" in which he laments that he had to "write his history from memory because native sources have been burnt by the enemy or put beyond his reach by circumstances." Tradition points to Flatholm island in the Bristol Channel as the place where he wrote his book.

Kentigern took the pilgrim's road to south Wales to seek out the saints David and Cadoc. It was the opportune place for refugee priests from the North to go. Cadoc had been active in Strathclyde, had educated Gildas and been confessor to his father. His monastery at Llancarfan near Cardiff was a natural rallying place. For these priests had not come looking for safety but for a chance to regroup with their allies and carry on the struggle more effectivly. The church of Llangyndeyrn near Carmarthen may commemorate Kentigern's exile in south Wales.†

Because of the tone of his book Gildas has sometimes been regarded as a bad tempered scold. But he had been driven from his homeland, seen its churches and holy books burned, friends killed and the life work of St. Ninian and of Arthur laid in ruins. He thought deeply on the causes of the disaster and then, dipping his pen in fire, he wrote like a Jeremiah, battling for his country and his cause.

By sharp contrasts he showed the gap between Christian life as it should be and the way it was being lived in Britain. His words blazed, burning the Bishops: "Monsters of ambition who buy for cash the office which should be earned by a holy life. They prance about haughtily, preaching alms but never giving a penny themselves. Judas in Peter's chair!" He scorched other Bishops for not reforming the situation: "The innocuous good, indolent in comfort."

His charges were well founded. A vacant bishopric had three rivals vying for it; one exploited his high birth, one gave lavish banquets and one made a deal with the electors to split the church property with them fifty-fifty.† That was in Gaul but there was similar corruption in Britain.

His words burned the "five evil kings": Constantine of Dumnonia; Aurelius of Gwent, "unworthy whelp of the lion" (Ambrosius); Votepori of Dyfed; Cinglas of Powis, "charioteer of the Bear"; and Maelgwn of Gwynedd, "The Island Dragon" and great-great-grandson of Cunedda. Upon Maelgwn fell the hottest coals of fire because he had been educated at Llanilltud and had become a monk until he saw an opportunity to seize the throne of Gwynedd. "Did you not vow yourself for ever a monk?" demanded Gildas. "We thought you had broken the nets in which fat bulls of your class get trapped by gold and your imperious will."

Some of his fiery arrows seem to have hit the mark. In Cornwall there is a church dedicated to St. Constantine, King of Dumnonia, who renounced his throne and went to work as a monk with Columcille, his distant cousin.

Gildas saw the monks as the one great hope, yet he was not gentle with them either: "You drink only water — but you quaff cups of hate. You measure out your bread — but boast about it without measure. Death enters through the window of pride."

The convictions he expressed were not his alone but were those of David and Cadoc, the ablest and most venerated teachers of the Celtic peoples. They were the tutors of St. Finnian of Clonard and the Irish had adopted a Mass and a Liturgy authored by these Welshmen. So the attack upon the Bishops could not have gone unnoticed across the sea in Ireland. Here too the hereditary Bishops suffered from the same sort of worldly infection. This may be the explanation why St. Finnian kept his own episcopal rank in the background and did not urge Columcille or the other Clonard men to become bishops.

The Destruction of Britain was important as history but its first significance was as a battle cry, rousing the Christian community, a Battle of Britain call to rise to their finest hour.

Strangely enough, Gildas never mentioned the rulers of his homeland of Strathclyde. Maybe he felt that the battle of the Faith in the North was irreparably lost. As Jocelyn's history put it, "The Christian religion in Strathclyde and Cumbria was almost entirely destroyed."

Only one small foothold in the North remained to Christianity. The Dalriad Scots, descendants of Lorn and Fergus macErc who had colonized Argyll in 500 AD, still clung to the faith of St. Patrick. Now upon them also fell the wrath of the heathens. The powerful and pagan Brude macMaelchon, High King of the Picts, attacked them in 559, killing their King Gabhran and seizing half their territory.

Dragons of Invergowrie.

The great war

Page of the Cathach — Battle Book — the psalter said to have been copied by St. Columba c. 560. At Royal Irish Academy.

Chapter twelve

The conflict which now engulfed Ireland was part of a wider war raging throughout the British Isles, in which Christianity was pitted against paganism. If this fact is kept in mind, much which seems confused becomes clear. Like all great wars, this one was mixed with lesser conflicts, cross purposes and odd alliances, yet overarching them all was one mighty issue: which faith would fail and which would go forward? In few wars has so much been at stake.

Every thrust and parry in this War of Faiths among the Britons produced repercussions in Ireland. The arrival of such refugees as King Rhydderch, the monks and nuns driven from Candida Casa and other victims of persecution spread alarm and foreboding among their Irish friends. Hope revived among the still powerful Druids and they went on the offensive, finding a rallying point for the pagan resurgence in the ancestral rites of Tara and the person of the *Ard Rí* Diarmit macCerbaill.

Diarmit was of the Southern Ui Neill, which had not accepted Christianity as fully as the Northern Ui Neill. Diarmit claimed Tara's sceptre in 544 AD, probably the year Columcille first declined it. Before that date he had been outlawed and Ciaran mac-an-tsaor befriended him and legend said that Diarmit helped drive in the first stakes for the chapel at Clonmacnois.

Gearoid MacNiocall described him thus: "Diarmit was almost certainly a pagan — and a sort of Christian also, who made obeisance to the Christian god when life was quiet but in times of stress called on the ancestral gods."†

unauthorised version was made of the Scriptures. It was to combat this danger that Rome later on adopted the system of "imprimatur".

Columcille however was a missionary leader in the forefront of a life and death battle and he was avid for any powerful new weapon. As he put the case, "It is not right to extinguish a Divine thing or prevent anyone copying, reading and circulating it."† A very Gaelic saying this was, claiming that wisdom was the inheritance of all the people.

Both men held valid viewpoints and there may have been an argument. Yet the urgency of the times must be remembered. If Jerome's text was to reach the Irish it must be circulated at once or it would be too late. Where were the Gospels and holy books of Strathclyde? Gildas had given the answer: "Burnt by the enemy." Is this what precipitated Columcille to action?

It is an oft-told tale that the dispute over the possession of the copy of the Gospel was appealed to *Ard Ri* Diarmit and that he gave judgment against Columcille with the words, "To every cow its calf and to every book its copy."

But this stretches credulity beyond all reason! The facts show how fantastic this tale is. According to the Canons of St. Patrick's Synod written about 550 AD, Christians were expressly warned to avoid the secular law courts with their Druidic oaths, and bring their complaints instead before the Church. Both Finbar and Columcille were "Bible Christians" and knew by heart St. Paul's stern rebuke to the Corinthians "How dare you go to law in a pagan court instead of laying your case before the saints?" In matters of faith, morals and discipline the Church has always reserved its right of judgement.

How totally inconceivable that a Christian Bishop and Abbot should take an ecclesiastical dispute before a Druid court. And it must be remembered that the *Ard Ri* was not a judge and the appeal would have been tried before the *Olave Brieve*, who was the Arch Druid macDe.†

No, there never was an appeal to the *Ard Ri*. If no appeal, then no verdict. If no verdict, then no cause for anger or desire for revenge. It is an invention.

How then did the tale arise? The likelihood seems strong that hostile people gleefully brought word of the dispute to Diarmit's attention. What a chance to sow dissension in the Christian ranks. What a chance for the *Ard Ri* to claim jurisdiction even over the internal affairs of the Church. What grand war propaganda!

It is important to notice that none of the earliest sources mention the copied Gospel incident. Neither Adomnan nor Bede allude to it nor do the Tighernach records which state that the ensuing war was caused by the King's muder of Prince Curnan.

King Diarmit helping St. Ciaran drive in the first stake at Clonmacnois. From the tenth century Cross of the Scriptures.

Columcille was forty years old when he faced the great crisis of his life, his trial by battle, and it divides his story into "before" and "after". For him it was the turning point, but no less it was the turning point for the Church in Ireland as well as for the great War of Faiths.

"The High King's judgement provoked Columcille's passionate nature to revenge." Such statements are found in many histories. So it is imperative to answer the question: is the Judgement-Vengeance legend credible? For this is the basis, and the only basis, for accusing Columcille of being violent, vindictive and blood-guilty. Examination of the facts has shown that the story of the *Ard Ri's* judgement is a myth. Will examination of the war also show that the story of revenge is fictitious?

Teltown, ten miles north of Tara, was the site of the Aenach, the Fair held in August every third year. Solemn sacrifices were offered, kings and brieves reviewed the laws, warriors competed in games. Gaels, always keen sportsmen, delighted in horse and chariot racing, greyhound coursing and in the fast and furious game of hurley, the parent game of hockey.

At the *Aenach* of 561 in a game of hurley, prince Curnan, son of Connaught's King Aed, struck an opposing player with his stick and killed him. He fled to Columcille and was granted the protection of Church sanctuary. During the past decades the Church's right of sanctuary had become recognized and the clergy were determined to maintain it.

Brehon law entitled Curnan to a trial and, if he paid the

blood-fine, to be pardoned. Nevertheless the *Ard Ri's* soldiers dragged him from sanctuary and murdered him.

Diarmit had violated a vital right of the Church — perhaps intentionally. But he had also broken the Law of the land which he had sworn to uphold. It was an act of lawless tyranny to which the Irish of that day would not submit. It meant war and King Aed called out the Connaught troops to avenge his son.

But the clans of the Northern Ui Neill, the Cenel Conaill and Cenel Eoghain, also rose in arms. The death of Curnan would mean little to them though they might resent the dishonouring of his protector. But there must have been a deeper cause.

The main strength of the Christians lay in the north among the Ulster and Connaught peoples for here St. Patrick had concentrated his work. Did they suspect that Diarmit and the Druids were out to crush the Christian tribes? This is how Dr. Lucy Menzies put it: "Columcille's followers regarded the battle as a test of power between Druidism and Christianity." This was the crunch of the matter. Though Columcille was in no sense in command, he was the focus of the Christian cause. It was this that made a show-down unavoidable. Was Ireland to go the way of Strathclyde? Would Columcille fail and fall like another Arthur?

His life threatened in Meath, Columcille fled alone by mountain trails, his knowledge of weather serving him well as he escaped his pursuers in the mists. It is said he took with him from St. Patrick's tomb, the Saint's prayer bell, both to preserve it from destruction and to help rouse the Christian tribes in the North. As he travelled to Donegal his thoughts took poetic form in "The Song of Trust":

> "God's elect are safe
> Even on the battlefront.
> No man can kill me before my day
> Even in close combat;
> No one can save me
> When the hour of death comes.
> No magic can tell my fate,
> No bird on twig or crooked oak.
> The voice of birds I do not idolise,
> Nor luck, nor love of son or wife.
> My druid is Christ, the Son of God."

Geography makes it clear that the northern clans did not attack the overlord, but that *Ard Ri* Diarmit was the aggressor. He invaded Connaught, marching his army right across Ireland to the ocean at Sligo Bay, aiming to cut King Aed off from his Ulster allies. At Culdremne between Sligo and Drumcliff he forced them to stand and give battle.

Tactically he chose a good position. The hunched mass of Ben Bulben Mountain crowds the northern road into a narrow pass beside the ocean. Victory here would stampede the Connaught-men to the south while the Ulstermen fell back to the north and both could be dealt with in detail. From the foot of Ben Bulben stretched moorland and here among the reed tufts and gorse Diarmit drew up his battle array, marching the troops three times round a cairn sunwise in the pagan *deasil* ceremony, while his Druids marked out an *airbhe,* a magical barrier round the army, that no enemy could cross and live.

In the Christian army the Connaughtmen served under

their King Aed, father of the murdered prince; Cenel
Eoghain was led by Domnall and Forcus, the sons of
Murcertach macErca, the first Christian *Ard Ri*: Cenel
Conaill was led by Columcille's cousin, Ainmire, King of
Donegal.

They chose for their standard a Psalter written in
Columcille's own hand, the famous *Cathach*, the Battle
Book. Treasured by the Cenel Conaill for centuries and
always borne before them in battle, it is now Ireland's
most ancient book and is preserved in the Royal Irish
Academy, Dublin. On that day in 561 at Culdremne when
the *Cathach* was trooped along the ranks, it was a symbol
of the Faith for which they fought.

The battle was short and decisive. Diarmit's army lost
3000 men; the Christian army had one man killed, because
he broke ranks against orders. The figure 3000 was often
used poetically by bards to indicate a large number and
may not be literal.

Victory was attributed to Columcille's prayers and
details of the action have not survived to explain why the
casualties were so one-sided. However, if Diarmit's men
felt the battle was a test of Druidic power, they may have
panicked when the *airbhe* failed to halt the enemy.

Any commander who bungled his battle as badly as
Diarmit might expect to lose his command or even his
head. But he did not even lose his sceptre, which argues a
powerful body of continuing support and also that the
victors did not follow up their victory by seeking vengeance on him.

The record of the war produced no evidence to support
the tale of Columcille's revenge. In the forty years before

the battle and the thirty-six years after it there is no incident of him acting vindictively. Why should it be thought that on this one occasion he acted out of character? It seems more reasonable to regard it as a surviving piece of war propaganda.

Culdremne was not much of a battle but it was a very decisive event. From then on Christianity held the initiative and the monastic saints became more and more the leaders and heroes of Ireland. For the Druids it had been the high water mark before their tide ebbed away.

Where tribal loyalties were so perfervid there were liable to be rifts, even in the Church. Not every Irish Bishop and cleric welcomed the teachings of Cadoc, Gildas and Finnian or approved of the dedicated men of Clonard. Some of these clergy convened a Synod at Teltown, no doubt reasoning that Columcille would not dare venture himself in hostile territory so near Tara. They voted to excommunicate him in absentia. Adomnan called the charges trifling and excusable.

Inconveniently Columcille came to the Synod anyway. As he entered only one man rose to greet him, Brendan of Birr, one of the "Twelve". There were angry shouts of remonstrance to which Brendan retorted, "I do not dare to slight the man fore-ordained by God to lead nations into life." Next on his feet was Bishop Finbar of Moville, proclaiming his affection and veneration for his former pupil. The vote of excommunication was withdrawn.

Here was an entirely new factor at work. The men of the monasteries had forged a higher loyalty than tribalism. At the Teltown Synod their unity passed the acid test. They stood together and they won.

Consequences were far-reaching. "The Canons show a monastic and an episcopal church existing side by side," wrote Dr. Kathleen Hughes, "though in the end the episcopal was thoroughly submerged. When and why did this unique change occur? It is generally accepted that it happened in the sixth century."†

The Teltown Synod points to a clue. Under pressure of the Druidic counterrevolution, many of the secular and hereditary clergy reverted to their local loyalties, more clansman than Christian. By contrast the monks, led by the Clonard group, held together in loyalty to Christ and each other. And as always in a crisis, leadership passed to the morally strong.

It is revealing to see how strategically Columcille placed his monasteries. Derry was in sight of Grianan of Ailech, seat of the kings of the Northern Ui Neill. Durrow was close to Uisneach, seat of the Southern Ui Neill. Kells was fifteen miles from Tara of the High Kings. Though he declined the sceptre himself, Columcille did not abdicate his responsibility for his own dynastic family. He was determined that the inspiration, wisdom and warning of the Church should be close at hand to his cousins who held the royal power.

There was a postscript to the battle of Culdremne which must be told although it does not directly concern Columcille. *Ard Ri* Diarmit learnt nothing from his defeat and in 563 his soldiers again dragged a fugitive from Church sanctuary and slew him. This time the victim was under the protection of St. Ruadhan, Abbot of Lothra, one of the "Twelve."

Ruadhan with his Bishop and clergy appeared on the green in front of Tara's palace where they sat down and began the ancient Celtic vigil of *Troscad*, fasting against an oppressor. This ritual protest is still practised in Iran and Mahatma Gandhi used it under the name of satyagraha in India.

Fasting and ringing their bells, the clergy kept their vigil, calling down on Tara a curse that "no king or queen should ever again live there." Then occurred an astonishing event. The people would not cross the saint's picket line; the ancient demi-god magic had faded from the name of *Ard Ri*. All supplies and services to the *Rath na Roigh* palace ceased. In desperation Diarmit was forced to abandon Tara saying, "Woe to him who contends with the Church!" The thousand-year-old enclosure was never occupied again.

In modern times Tara has been mourned sentimentally but in its own day it does not seem to have inspired much affection. A more contemporary view, although a churchman's, is contained in lines, freely rendered, from a poem of Angus the Culdee about 800 AD:

"Tara is dead and all its princes gone;
Great Armagh and its singing choirs lives on.
Aileen's proud, boasting host are flown,
Victorious Cruachan is only ruined stone,
Yet royal grace shines upon Clonmacnois.
Mountains of evil felled like rotted trees;
God's Kingdom fills the earth, the heavens, the seas."

Two years later in 565 AD Diarmit came to his own end. The place of his death, at Rathbeg near Antrim town in the land of the Cruithne, implied that he was again the aggressor. The legend that has survived is full of myth and magic. Against the warning of his Queen, the High King went to a wild party at Banban's Inn where one by one he transgressed all his *gessa* and so was doomed. Finally the inn was surrounded by his enemies who set it on fire and as he dashed for the door he met Black Aed macSuibne of the Cruithne royal house. "This is your way out", shouted Aed and thrust his spear through the King. Mortally wounded, he fell back into a huge vat of ale and the burning roof fell on him. Thus he died the three-fold death so beloved by the bards: *guin, badud, loscad* — wounding, drowning, burning.

Whatever did happen, it seems to be a fact that Diarmit was killed by Black Aed. "The death of Diarmit", wrote Francis J. Byrne, "signalised the demise of the pagan sacral Kingship of Tara and produced a period of considerable confusion."†

Bell of St. Ruadhan of Lothra, now at Limerick.

The tide of victory was running in Ireland, it was a time to be bold and launch new ventures. To a statesman's eye it was evident that sooner or later a beach-head of the Faith had to be established across the sea in north Britain. But who would do it, when, where and how?

Comgall of Bangor and Brendan the Sailor had both explored the possibilities in the Hebrides but their attempts to plant monastic colonies there had been wiped out by pirates who infested the sea lanes. Comgall at Bangor was already planning a new attempt and soon afterwards his cousin St. Moluag left to found his settlement at Lismore. Columcille conferred with both of them and others of the "Twelve". Up to now Irishmen had gone abroad to receive training and then returned to work among their own people. The Clonard men proposed something entirely new; to send companies of Irishmen overseas to combat paganism in its own strongholds.

Off the Galway coast of Ireland lay the Aran Isles on which St. Enda (d.530), a monk from Candida Casa, had founded a training school which produced many generations of saints and leaders. In this inspiring place Columcille spent several months pondering his course of action.

At this precise juncture came a call for help from King Conall of the Dalriad Scots in Argyll. His little kingdom, still Christian, was under imminent threat from the northern Picts. That Conall in his trouble turned for help to his cousin Columcille, rather than to some war lord, marks him as a man of vision. He did not appeal in vain.

The opportunity he was praying for had come and

Columcille recognized it at once as God's destiny. His whole life had been a preparation for this. The risks were high and once committed there could be no turning back but, God willing, he would go to the help of the Scots.

Adomnan recorded his motive as *"pro Christo peregrinari volens* — pilgrimage for the love of Christ." Pilgrimage was an essential part of monastic philosophy, always linked with missionary action. From the early days of the Desert Fathers monks left behind their native heath to imitate Abraham who left his homeland "desiring a better country, that is, a heavenly." St. Patrick witnessed to "a love of God so intense that I might part with fatherland and kinfolk". The monks' term for this missionary going forth was "exile", but it carried no thought of punishment but rather was regarded as a glorious witness, undertaken for the love of God and His children. The Middle-Irish "Life of Columcille" sets out his doctrine: "These are they of the perfect pilgrimage who say 'I give Thee thanks for it, O God; I have pilgrimage and exile in the world even as the elders who went before'"

Adomnan was a statesman and well understood, as had the saint, the strategic importance of the Iona mission in converting the north of Britain. But he preferred to record the supreme motive that underlay the actions of all monks, "for the love of Christ".

To go with him on this dangerous operation Columcille picked twelve companions, following Christ's example. All were his relatives. As second-in-command he chose Baithen macBrenainn, his first cousin and fosterson; Cobach, Baithen's brother; Ernan, his own uncle; Mochonna, a king's son; Diarmit, his personal servant;

Rue and Fechno who were brothers, Scandal, Echoid, Tochann, Cairann and Grilaan.

Columcille tried to send young Mochonna back to his father. "You are my father, the Church is my mother and my country is where I can harvest men for Christ!" exploded Mochonna and that settled the argument. Before sailing, Columcille visited Bishop Finbar. The old man was sitting in the evening sun outside his chapel when he saw his favourite pupil approaching. "Look at Columcille," he said, "Heaven has deemed him worthy to have an angel for a companion on his wanderings."

Late in April 563 AD the "Island Soldiers", as Columcille called his company, loaded their ship for the voyage. Her name it seems was *Liath Bailidh* — the Mayor's Grey. Other books say she was the *DEARG DRUCHTCH*† — "Dewy Red" — but that was probably a ship he used twenty years later. She was a sea-worthy curragh such as is still sailed off the West Coast of Ireland. She was not, as some have said, "a frail coracle". The freight she carried was light; some cooking pots, farm tools, seed, altar linen and a few books and little else but faith. They cast off from Derry, sailed out of Lough Foyle, coasting to Rathlin Island and across the dozen miles of open sea to Kintyre. Navigation in those days was mainly visual, steering from landmark to landmark.

They are said to have landed on Kintyre in Scotland at Southend. On the impressive cliffs above the sea, cut in the rock, is "St. Columba's Footprint".

Angus McVicar, the Kintyre historian and author, says "The Footprint dates from before Christ, probably used by Chiefs to pledge their faith to the tribe. But I think

Columcille did use it, for he was a statesman as well as a missionary and it was his principle to base the new teaching on the foundation of the old. He would pay homage to the beliefs of the tribe by putting his foot in the print."

The next port of call was Delgon at the head of Loch Killisport where they were joyfully welcomed and entertained by Conall, King of Dalriada. In the cave they used as a chapel during their stay can still be seen the altar and the Cross that they carved on the wall above it.

With the King they discussed the most strategic site for their missionary outpost and no doubt he spoke of the Island of Iona. He knew it well as his father, grandfather and great-grandfather were buried there.

Off the west coast of the mainland of Alban lay the large island of Mull which stretched a long leg of land down to the south-west. At the end of the leg, like a kicked off shoe, was the island of Iona, three and a half miles long and a mile wide. Its location was politically ideal as it was on the boundary between Dalriada and the Picts. It was within easy rowing distance of the mouth of the Great Glen which led to the Pictish capital of Inverness.

When Columcille left King Conall he seems to have sailed up the Sound of Islay, thereby avoiding the dangerous whirlpool of Corryvreckan at the northern tip of Jura. Tradition tells that they put in to the small island of Oronsay. From there it was twenty miles across the open sea to Iona.

Iona was an obvious choice in so many ways. Being an island gave it protection but being only a mile off the coast of Mull it was not remote or isolated. The coastal trade route passed it and ships used a nearby anchorage. The Scots already reverenced it as the burial place of their Kings.

Yet around the choice of Iona has twined a tangle of myths which need to be unravelled. The story goes that Columcille was condemned, or condemned himself to perpetual exile in penance supposedly for causing the killing at Culdremne. Adomnan and Bede knew nothing about this and there is no reliable evidence to support it. Columcille severed no ties and surrendered no jurisdiction over his Irish monasteries and he returned to Ireland quite freely on at least ten occasions.

Yet the tale persists and draws its main support from the romantic tale of *Cairn Cul Ri Erin*. Columcille and his men, it is claimed, landed first on the island of Oronsay but found that Ireland was still in sight. Being doomed nevermore to see his homeland, the "exile" sailed on to Iona and, finding that Ireland was no longer in sight, decided to stay. A cairn of stones was erected on a hill and called *Cul Ri Erin* — Back to Ireland.

There are cairns called *Cul Ri Erin* on both Oronsay and Iona. There is also such a cairn on the mountainside of Ben More on Mull, east of Iona. Here the *Cairn Cul Ri Erin* is matched by another called *Cairn Cul Ri Alban* — Back to Scotland. This clearly indicates the original purpose of these cairns. The northern half of Mull was owned by the Picts of Alban; the southern half was owned by the Dalriad Scots from Ireland. The cairns notified that "behind this point the land belongs to the Picts of Alban" or "to the Irish of Dalriada." The boundary line passed through the island of Iona.

The presence of a boundary cairn on Iona explains the apparent contradiction between the records of Tighernach, an Irish monk, and of the Anglo-Saxon monk Bede. "King Conall immolated the island of Hii (Iona) to Columcille", is the entry in Tighernach. But Bede said, "The island belongs to the realm of Britain. The Picts who inhabit these districts donated it." As it was on the border, both Picts and Scots had property claims and the newcomers had to clear their title with both of them.

There is an ancient poem inscribed "Columcille fecit" which so remarkably describes the scene from the *Cul Ri Erin* hill, that is hard to doubt that it was written on the spot, though it is attributed to the Twelfth Century. The poet speaks of *Uchd Ailiun*, hill of the meadow, and this hill rises from the meadow where the monks pastured their cattle. In part it says:

> "What joy to be on Uchd Ailiun
> On the pinnacle of rock
> Often to hear the waves sing to their Father,
> The roar of the sea in ebb and flow
> Beside the church; no sorrow this!
> Were Cul Ri Erin my mystic name,
> Contrite for sin, I'd look at her,
> Yet bless the Lord Who saves us all."

The poem continues in joyous praise. The poet knew of the cairn but gives no hint of connecting it with agonizing remorse. This is the song of a pilgrim but not of a grieving, homesick exile.

The tradition that Columcille climbed to the top of Uchdachan soon after he landed could well be true. It was the

The rock of Dunadd, fortress capital of the Scots in Argyll. At its summit the author places his foot in the Royal Footprint where Kings pledged to walk in their ancestors' steps.

Cave at Killisport, Argyll used as a chapel by Columcille when he first landed in Scotland.

best way to get an over-all view of the island and to select a good site for the monastery.

How did the myth of exile arise? Perhaps through a misunderstanding of the special monastic use of the word "exile". Or perhaps Columcille's enemies, delighted to see him leave Ireland, set a rumour of exile in circulation which with the passage of time has petrified into "popular history".

There is no dishonour about being exiled for one's faith; it happened to St. Kentigern and St. Gildas. But the historical fact seems to be that Columcille never was exiled.

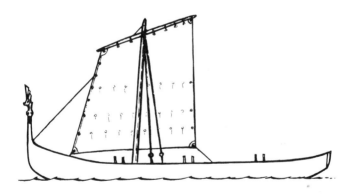

The Iona Curragh sailed from Derry to Iona in 1963 for the 1400th centenary celebrations. It was skippered by Wallace Clark of N. Ireland. In 1976 a leather-sheathed Curragh of this type was built by Dr. Tim Severin and sailed with a crew of four from Ireland to Canada, weathering Atlantic gales and the Labrador ice-pack.

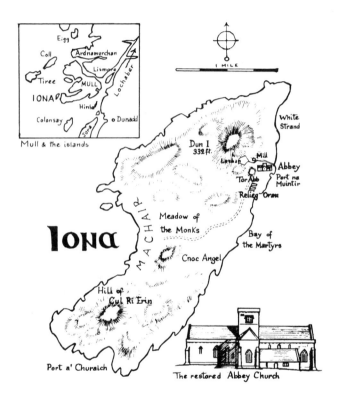

Mull & the islands

1 MILE

IONA

MACHAIR

White Strand

Dun I
332 ft.

Mill

Abbey
Port na
Muintir

Tor Abb

Relieg Oran

Meadow of
the Monks

Bay of
the Martyrs

Cnoc Angel

Hill of
Cul Ri Erin

Port a' Churaich

The restored Abbey Church

On the Eve of Whitsun, May 12th, 563 AD the bow of the curragh grounded on the beach at Port a' Churaich at the south end of Iona. The pounding of the waves in this exposed bay has burnished the red, green and black pebbles to gem-like lustre. The bay is ringed by barren, uninviting hills but even more uninviting were the party of men who came over the heights to confront Columcille and his Island Soldiers. They were led by two bishops who curtly demanded that they all leave the island by the way they had come.

These must have been hereditary heirs of the collegiate group of seven bishops that are known to have been on Iona some generations earlier. Columcille was polite but firmly refused to recognize them as bishops in any true sense and he made his point so convincingly that they withdrew their opposition.

Next the monks explored the sheltered east coast and three quarters of the way up the island found a suitable landing place close to level pasture and here the Abbot decided to build a monastery. Six hundred yards inland rose the craggy hill of Dun-1, 332 feet high, providing protection from north-westerly gales. At its foot was a small lake from which ran a stream with enough flow to turn a mill.

Once the site was pegged out the men began to dig the *rath*, a rampart to enclose their new home. The meadow was gay with primroses, daisies, wild hyacinth, thyme and buttercups and larks went skyward shouting encouragement, while oyster-catchers sped back and forth along the beaches. This was the chosen spot to which they had been led to fulfill God's purpose. Yet had they been seeking a place solely for its beauty they could have found nowhere more glorious. Columcille's saying is still true, "Iona lays a blessing on every eye that sees it."

Another strange fable about their arrival illustrates how time and superstition can corrode truth into fantastic shapes. "Columcille thus said to his people," runs an ancient Irish tale, "It would be well for us that our roots pass into the earth here. It is permitted that one of you go under the earth to consecrate it.' Oran arose and spoke, 'I am ready for that.' He lay down and went to Heaven."†

In reality St. Oran was a missionary from Latteragh, Tipperary, who founded churches on Colonsay, Tiree and Mull before dying on Iona of bubonic plague in the epidemic of 549 AD, fourteen years before Columcille arrived at the island.

Though refusing to recognize the hereditary bishops, Columcille was swift to honour his missionary predecessor and may have said, "It is well for us that our roots already run under the earth consecrating it." But the pagan belief that *buada* demanded a sacrificial victim be buried under a new building, lingering on in folklore, distorted St. Oran's story into this bizarre form.

Adomnan did not know the tale and reported that the first of the Brethren to be buried at Iona was Brito, a Briton, who died of natural causes. The island graveyard is still called *Reilig Oran* and in it lie 48 Kings of Scots, 4 Irish and 7 Norse Kings.

At one place on the Island a modern pilgrim feels specially close to that shipload of pioneers. It is in the wild and lonely beauty of the Bay of the Curragh where they landed. Tradition has claimed that they buried the ship here under a grassy mound. Perhaps the old ship worked hard for many years but at last ceased to be seaworthy. But how could the Brethern break her up? How natural and human if they brought her back to the Bay where they had landed and gave her honourable burial.

Iona differed little in appearance or administration from all the other Celtic monasteries. Inside the *rath* the main building was the church, constructed of oak rafted over from Mull because few trees grew on Iona. Around it clustered the wattle and thatch *botha* of the monks and facing the west door of the church on top of a rocky hillock called Tor-Abb, was the Abbot's cell which commanded a wide view over the straits. The *Proinntigh* was a large building where all had their meals, served from a great flat rock called *Blathnat*, the sharing stone. It is still there. Bread and milk, fish and eggs were the daily diet with some mutton, beef, or seal meat on Sundays, Feast Days or for guests.

The Brethren wore tunics with hooded cowls of undyed wool over them. As the sheep of those days were black, the cowls were dark in colour. Only Abbots wore white cowls. Sandals were worn out of doors and the ancient courtesy of washing a guest's feet was observed. All monks who had taken vows received the Celtic tonsure, shaving the hair on the forehead from ear to ear while letting it grow at the back. This tonsure appears to have been adopted from the *Filidh*.

For the work of the monastery the Brothers were divided into Seniors, Working Brothers and Alumni. The duty of the Seniors was to conduct five daily services, Vespers, Prime, Tierce, Sext, None; to educate the Alumni (Students); and to copy the Scriptures, a vital task to put more Bibles into circulation.

Younger, fitter men worked the farm, fished, milled and cooked. Iona was 2000 acres in size but only a third could be cultivated and most of the good machair land was along the western shore. So in those first days the Island Soldiers marched out at dawn singing, armed with the *caschrom*, foot plough, to break the soil and put in a crop. It was a week's work for a man to plough an acre, but they had no draught animals to begin with.

Some monks did special work: a butler, a cook, a baker (Genereus was English), a smith, a miller, a gardener; and there were 60 rowers to man the boats; the community grew to about two hundred people connected with the Abbey.

> "Wonderful the warriors who abode in Hii
> Thrice fifty in the monastic rule.
> With their boats along the ocean
> Three score men a-rowing."

Hospitality was a sacred duty alike to Gael and Christian, so the *Tighaoidheadha*, guest house, was one of the abbot's personal cares and many were the anecdotes of his princely courtesy as a host.

> "I saw a stranger yesterday;
> I put food in the eating place.
> Drink in the drinking place,

> Music in the listening place:
> And in the Name of the Trinity
> He blessed me and my house,
> My cattle and my dear ones.
> And the lark said in her song
> Often, often, often
> Goes Christ in the stranger's guise."

But details about Iona should not obscure its audacious aim — to establish a colony of Heaven upon the earth. Many have dreamt that dream and many still do. Some have tried to build it through philosophies, by plans or by laws, even by violence, with God or without Him. At the end of his life Khrushchev admitted, "The contradictions in the Communist society have their cause in the inability to create a selfless man."

A selfless man — that was Columcille's starting point in all he was and did. A re-made world needs to be populated by re-made people. Man's nature is selfish but God's nature is to change man by a miracle. Columcille and his men had experienced that change and they believed in miracles for the best of reasons: they *were* miracles. It was their delight to serve God and so they selflessly served His children also.

To the neighbouring Picts and Scots everything about the Iona colony must have seemed upside down. They were used to social strata of noble and servile classes. And they judged all behaviour by that favourite Gaelic phrase *Is coir* — it is fitting, not necessarily good or bad but proper, the "done thing". It was fitting for kings to give gold rings, for *Filidh* to sing to the harp, for warriors to drink in the mead hall and it was not fitting for a noble's wife to milk a cow.

What a social revolution these monks stirred up! The majority of them came from the noble and learned classes. What would the neighbours say when they saw the noble Baithen hoeing or Mochonna sweating with a foot-plough or the Abbot himself, a prince of the Blood Royal, humping grain sacks to the mill on his own back. *Ni coir ar bit* — not fitting at all. Yet these strange and happy men elevated manual work — odious symbol of the servile class — to the glory of a priestly offering to God.

When the Island Soldiers sallied out into the countryside the farmers learnt that they did not have to hide their cattle and daughters in the woods. The monks shared what they had instead of plundering; set people free instead of seizing hostages, skilfully healed the sick but demanded no reward. It was all so new, so opposite to the old ways.

The monks ate sparingly, not just for the sake of their own souls. It was their protest and witness against the gross gluttony and drinking of the rich few in a land where most children always went to bed hungry. It might be fitting for warriors to gorge on the *Curath Mir,* but the monks chose instead to share the slaves' diet.

But every Sunday all work stopped and the Island Soldiers gathered for their Feast when every warrior was awarded the Hero's Portion, the broken Bread and poured out Wine.

Although the Rule of Columcille belongs to a later century, some of its articles reveal how the Island Soldiers trained themselves to be spiritually hardy.

> "Be naked (stripped of material possessions) in imitation of Christ.

"No idle words; at once give God's speed to a tattler.

"Pray for those who trouble you.

"Forgiveness from the heart for everyone.

"Eat only when hungry; sleep only when sleepy.

"Three labours: Prayer — Work — Reading.

"Work; your own needs — your share of others' needs — help for your neighbours.

"A mind prepared for Red Martyrdom (to die for Christ).

"A mind fortified for White Martyrdom (to live and witness for Him).

"Pray till the tears come; work till the sweat comes.

"Almsgiving above all else."

"The hopeless corruption of the surrounding pagan society", wrote Professor Skene, "showed in its utter disregard for the sanctity of domestic ties and in its unjust, selfish, violent, bloody character. By contrast the monks exhibited a life of purity, holiness and self-denial." Iona became an open court of equity and mercy, a stronghold of honour, to which fled the victims of violence and the fugitives from justice. Both received fair and firm dealing from the Abbot. Whoever came to the island was welcomed under the Law of the Church: "The enslaved shall be freed, the plebian exalted through service to God. For the Lord will not refuse any man, therefore the Church is open to all."

Picts and Scots watched and wondered as the Kingdom of Heaven took form in their midst and a new light chased the gloom from the glens and sea locks of the Hebrides.

Pictish symbols whose meaning remains a mystery.

For the first two years the Brothers worked quietly on the island, preaching by doing, showing what it meant to live as citizens of Heaven. Two thirds of the incidents related by Adomnan in his book took place on Iona but as they are not in any chronological order, it is impossible to be sure when they happened. But some look as if they belong to this early period. Adomnan's vivid stories show us Columcille at work day by day among the Gaels and Picts who were his neighbours.

Findchan, the farmer at Dalcros, was the sort of grouchy man who makes it hard "to love thy neighbour". The Iona monks had been granted the right to cut wattles in Dalcros bay and they rowed over to collect several boat loads for construction of the Guest House. Findchan, whose land adjoined the bay, was very angry about it.

To placate him, Columcille sent over three measures of seed barley with the message, "Sow it and trust God". This made the farmer more angry than ever. "How can a crop succeed when it is already past mid-summer?" he raged. But his wife soothed him down. "Why don't you do as the good Abbot says?" she suggested. So the farmer put the barley in and to his amazement reaped a fine crop early in August. The food was welcome but the real gift was that Findchan learned to trust God.

On his travels through Mull Columcille met an old woman gathering nettles and asked her why she was doing it. "O darling father," she answered, "I have only one cow and she is with calf. So till she drops her calf I must live on nettle soup."

Rations were short at the monastery and the Abbot had nothing to send her but he called his servant Diarmit and told him, "Nettle soup for me, only nettle soup from now on. As long as the old woman has to live on that, I will too."

Diarmit, the devoted family retainer, was determined that the Abbot must keep up his strength. So he took his spurtle, stirring stick, and bored a hole through the length of it. Then he attached a skin bag to the top and filled it with beef broth. He hid the bag up his sleeve and as he stirred the nettle soup the beef broth ran through the hollow spurtle and enriched it. No doubt the Abbot was amused that he had been hoodwinked.

Columcille travelled widely through Mull, in the wilds of Ardnamurchan, across to Skye and up the Great Glen into Lochaber. He visited Ardnamurchan four times in the first two years. All was Pict country. He met the chiefs, befriended the poor, cured the sick, baptised the children and the people came to know and trust him.

Among the Picts of Lochaber there was a well, haunted by evil spirits and dreaded by the country folk who said its water caused blindness, leprosy and insanity. Columcille walked up to the well and made over it "The Saving Sign", as he called the Cross, much as an explorer might plant the flag, claiming the territory for his King. Then he washed his hands and face and drank some of the water.

The curious crowd watched to see if he would be stricken. But he was unscathed and announced to the people that henceforth it was a holy well under the protection of Christ and would become a blessing to the community.

Pioneer missionaries in heathen countries have rarely been naïve about the powers of evil, of witchcraft and magic. St. Patrick prayed to be kept safe "Against snares of demons, against black laws of heathenry, against spells of women, smiths and Druid." They acknowledged that the sorcerers had powers but maintained that Christ was more powerful.

A pagan's whole existence was dogged by fear of evil spirits; they lurked in every shadow, behind every bush, in any unusual happening. For protection he turned to incantations and each daily act demanded some magic spell and woe if the right words were forgotten.

Fear is a liar and Columcille struck at the root of its tyranny. He wrote poems about the everyday things, set them to music and sent the Picts and Gaels out to face the perils of the day singing these prayers of praise. They became the folksongs of the Highlands and some have lasted till today.

> "Traversing corries and forest wild
> Down winding glen, up mountain side
> The fair white Mary still uphold me,
> The shepherd Jesus be my guide."

Adomnan told twenty anecdotes about Columcille working among the Picts: baptising a gallant old warrior chief in Skye, helping a pauper at Loch Lochy to snare food for his family, comforting a farmer from Loch Rannoch with word that his family was safe. It is evident why he was known to them as "the kind Columcille". Yet some authors have said that he was scornful and hostile towards the Picts, a view contradicted by Adomnan's record.

Nesan-the-Crooked in Lochabar was a poor Pict who had only five cows but he joyfully entertained the Abbot. Columcille blessed his cattle, predicting that they would increase to a hundred and five. But Vigenus was rich and stingy and turned the monks away from his door, and almost unheard of discourtesy among Celts. "In spurning guests he has spurned Christ," said Columcille and, with insight into cause and effect in human nature, added, "He will be reduced to nothing and his son will run from door to door with a half-empty bag". And that is what happened to each man.

On the rugged peninsula of Ardnamurchan Columcille became friends with a struggling Pict farmer called Colman. He too had only five cows and so the Abbot told him the story about Nesan-the-Crooked and his herd. "If you will bless my cows I know they will increase," answered Colman.

Columcille discovered why hardworking Colman was so poor. Ten miles off the coast of Ardnamurchan was the isle of Coll, lair of a pirate gang of Gaelic ruffians. They were led by two brothers, Ioan and Conall nicknamed *Lamb Deas* — Right Hand, who were descended from Gabhran the late king of Dalriada. Twice these pirates had sacked Colman's farm and he had started again from nothing.

In this affair Columcille clashed head-on with the accepted economic system of the day, the economics of plunder. He, a prince of the Gaels, boldly opposed fellow Gaels, his own kinsmen, in defence of a Pict.

Ioan the pirate raided Colman's farm once again but on the way back to his ship he met Columcille, who appealed to him to give back his loot. The argument went on so long that Columcille waded out into the glassy calm sea right to the pirate's boat. But Ioan would not relent and rowed away, leaving Columcille still calling after him. As the Abbot waded ashore he remarked, "He won't get back to his fellow ruffians. There'll be a violent squall soon."

Understanding weather, he knew that a glassy calm on a hot morning presaged one of those sudden Hebridean squalls. Sure enough, a storm struck the pirates when they were half way across the straits to Coll and the boat went down with all hands.

Lamh Deas blamed Columcille for the squall and the death of his brother and vowed revenge. Some time later the Abbot and his men were travelling through Lochaber and in the evening beached their boat at an abandoned village and settled down in the huts for the night. At midnight Columcille roused them, and telling them to carry the boat along, climbed the hillside and camped in the open. In the dead of night the thatch of the village huts burst into flames.

A Highland custom which immigrants brought to Canada, was still being observed within living memory. The left shoe was always put on first then the right shoe; after that the left shoe was laced and tied, then the right shoe. Tradition claimed that Columcille and his men were once ambushed at night and fled without time to put on their shoes. They blundered into a big patch of nettles and were badly stung. Thereafter the Abbot adopted this sensible drill for putting shoes on in a hurry. This could be a folk memory of the perilous days when Columcille was hounded by pirates in the glens of Lochaber.

The Abbot excommunicated Lamh Deas for robbery and murder. The pirate tracked him to the small island monastery of Hinba where he often withdrew to meditate. But the monk Finlugan saw Lamh Deas landing and guessed that he had come to assassinate the saint. He snatched up the Abbot's cowl which was white unlike those of the monks. He put it on, ready to die in his stead. The ruse fooled the murderer who hurled his spear at Finlugan but it passed through the white cowl without hurting the monk. The pirate fled to his boat convinced that he had made an end of his holy kinsman. About a year later someone with a better aimed spear made an end of Conall Lamh Deas.

On Ardnamurchan Colman's herd increased until it reached one hundred and five head. It never grew any bigger than the number promised by Columcille. The reason was that whenever his herd exceeded 105, Colman gave the extra cattle to charity. "And he rendered many goodly services," recorded Adomnan.

Pictish symbols

"The Kingdom of God does not consist in persuasive arguments but in a clear demonstration of power", once declared St. Ambrose, the great Doctor of the Church. The time had come for Columcille to advance out of the beach-head and, accepting extreme risks, strike a decisive blow by a demonstration of power.

The news from the rest of Britain was threatening and there was no time to lose. After a forty-year lull the Saxons were on the march again. The West Saxons had captured Salisbury. The Orkney pirates, in collusion with the Lowland Picts, were raiding as of old. King Ida of Northumbria from his stronghold named Bamburgh, after his wife Bebba, was forcibly extending his dominion north and west. Meanwhile Britannia, torn by squabbling factions, was a tempting prey.

Therefore in 565 AD Columcille determined to visit the High King of the Picts. No friendly reception was to be expected because the Picts were both pagans and enemies of the Gaels. Six years earlier they had attacked them and driven them out of half the Dalriad colony. The High King might well resent the priests at Iona establishing themselves on his frontier without his consent.

Brude macMaelchon, the High King, was a formidable man to face, the most powerful monarch ever to rule the Picts of Alban. His territory extended from the Firth of Forth to Cape Wrath and he was overlord also of the Orkneys. Brude was a royal name which alternated with others like Nechtan, Drust and Talorc in the Pictish Kings' Lists. He himself had inherited the throne by right of his mother in accordance with the matri-linear succession laws of the Picts.

The Royal Ladies, through whom the sovereignty descended, often chose their consorts outside the nation of Picts. To a Roman matron who sneered at the custom, a Pictish princess retorted, "You Roman women consort in secret with the vilest of men. We consort in public with the noblest."

Brude macMaelchon's mother almost certainly chose King Maelgwn of Gwynedd in north Wales to be the father of her son. A cultivated man who encouraged poetry and art at his Court at Degannwy, he had been in his youth a monk, a fact bluntly pointed out by St. Gildas. However, Brude macMaelchon, child of this union, was brought up and educated with his mother's people in the land of the Picts and may never have met his father.

Columcille called on his two best friends to go with him on this audacious approach to the Picts; Comgall, Abbot of Bangor, and Kenneth, later Abbot of Achabo. They were just the men to relish a risky adventure and as both were Irish Cruithne akin to the Picts, they were ideal ambassadors.

Brude macMaelchon's capital was near Inverness, probably within the limits of the present city. To reach it the three Abbots faced a hundred-mile boat journey through hostile territory. They sailed in Dalriad waters as far as Lismore, the slim ten-mile-long island in the mouth of Loch Linnhe. Most probably they then conferred with Comgall's cousin Moluag who was founding his missionary outpost here. He was to play a vital role in the follow-up of this bold strategy. From there on they were in

Pict country, rowing up the narrowing funnel of Loch Linnhe, where Ben Nevis loomed above them; through the river into Loch Lochy and by Invergarry into Loch Ness which led like a broad avenue straight to their destination.

When the Abbots arrived before the royal fortress they found the gates barred against them by order of the King; Columcille walked up to the great folding doors, made the sign of the Cross and knocked. Adomnan recorded, "The bolts were driven back with great force" and the Abbots walked in.

Was there a guard on duty whose family had been befriended by the monks who, at the risk of his life, pulled back the bolts? What does it matter whether God touched the bolts or the heart of a guard? It was a miracle.

They had gained entrance and also gained the King's attention. Shocked to hear that the priests were already inside the walls, the King hurried from his palace to give them a respectful welcome and during the discussions that followed he paid them the compliment of removing his sword, to show that they had won his complete confidence.

Adomnan's account does not say that Brude macMaelchon was baptised, but Bede's history, the Pictish Chronicle and the Life of St. Comgall both say that he was baptised in the 8th year of his reign, 565 AD. Of course, if he was the son of Maelgwn of Gwynedd he may already have received infant baptism as part of the marriage agreement.

Some historians have suggested that the Abbots' mission was a failure because no land appears to have been given for a church near the royal residence, as was the usual custom. However, Comgall's disciple St. Moluag of Lismore was soon given land for a monastery at Rosemarkie at the mouth of the Inverness Firth. Being a Cruithne he was a most suitable man to head up the missionary work among the Picts. Monasteries like Mortlach show the spread of his work along the Moray coast. Isabel Henderson has observed "Some of the most distinguished of the later Cross-slabs are found in Moray and Ross. One wonders if this rich flowering of Christian art had its origin in some important ecclesiastical foundation established at the time of the Columban mission."

Columcille himself became King Brude's *amn chara* —soul friend, and remained so for twenty years. This specifically Christian term could hardly have been applied to Brude if he had remained a pagan.

While the three Abbots were at Inverness, the roving sailor St. Cormac O'Lethan was at sea heading for the Orkneys. He must have synchronized his voyage with the Abbots' visit to the Picts. The Orkney pirates had terrorized the British coasts for two centuries and Cormac's mission was highly dangerous. Columcille urged Brude, as overlord of the Islands, to instruct the rulers there that nothing untoward happen to him. Brude gave the command and it did in fact save Cormac's life.

Not everyone at Inverness welcomed the monks. Arch Druid Broichan, chief adviser and foster father of Brude, used all his political and magical skill to thwart them. One night at the palace the Abbots were singing Vespers when the Druids raised a racket to drown out their voices.

When needed, Columcille's magnificent singing voice
had the power of a trumpet and that night he let go full
volume with the 45th Psalm, hushing foe and friend in
awe.

> "My heart overflows with a worthy theme.
> I address my verses to the King.
> My tongue is the pen of a ready writer."

When finally the Abbots prepared to leave for home,
Broichan asked Columcille, "When do you propose to
sail?" He replied, "In three days' time, God willing."
"Aha, you won't be able to!" cried Broichan, "I can make
adverse winds and a great darkness." Columcille answered,
"God rules everything and He is directing our
movements."

The day came and the Druids gathered gleefully on the
shore to watch the Christians' discomforture, as a black
squall scudded up Loch Ness. The boat's crew hesitated
but Columcille, a skilled sailor, stepped aboard, took the
steering oar and pushed off. Holding the boat close to the
wind, he raced into the storm in a glory of spray. The
squall passed as suddenly as it had come and he had good
sailing down the Loch.

Courage, good seamanship but above all instant obedience, that when God says, "Go", you go, and leave the
outcome to Him. If the Druids thought they had seen a
miracle they were not far wrong.

The case of Broichan interestingly reveals Columcille's
way of dealing with an enemy. The Arch Druid had lost
his politcal pull with the High King but worse, he had
discovered to his dismay that all his hard-learned arts of
necromancy were powerless. His life was in ruins and if he

suffered a nervous breakdown it would not be surprising. He was convinced that his end was near when he saw an apparition, causing him to drop a precious glass goblet from which he was drinking, and found he could only breathe with difficulty.

Columcille and his party were camping by Loch Ness when two mounted men galloped up with a message from King Brude, begging him to save the life of Broichan who was dying. A vindictive man would have answered, "Serve him right."

However, Columcille did two things which showed a wise insight into human nature. On the shore of Loch Ness he had picked up a white stone which floated — possibly pumice. He sent Broichan this curious pebble, telling him to put it in water and then drink the water. Like Elisha curing the leprosy of Naaman (II Kings Ch. 5), he did not attribute medicinal properties to the water, but he knew that faith begins with the first step of obedience. Faith would heal. Secondly, he commanded Broichan to set free a Scots girl whom he had kidnapped. Unless moral change began, the Druid's change of heart would not last long and he would die spiritually and physically.

This was how the Abbot of Iona practised "love your enemy" with a Druid. Broichan obeyed, set free his concubine, was cured and became a firm friend. A man who could thus turn enemies into friends had no need to smite them dead with anathemas. This is the true answer to those who persist in calling Columcille "violent".

The strength of his idea and the magnetism of his example were so powerful that he had no need for violence. Later ages invented fairy tales of withering hands or turning people into cranes. But as Brude laid aside his sword, so Columcille had the power to disarm the violence and hostility of others.

The expedition to Inverness achieved many far-reaching results. The Brethren of Iona were confirmed in their tenure of the island. The survival of the Kingdom of the Scots of Dalriada was assured. The whole northern flank of the pagan alliance was detached. The land of the Picts was opened up to the preaching and teaching of Christian missionaries. And although the three Abbots could not have guessed it, a process of friendly merging between the northern peoples was begun which in the fullness of time created the Scottish nation.

The Pictish Beast:
the Meigle stone.

Chapter nineteen

Down in South Wales the same War of the Faiths was being waged by a growing force of determined Christians who had rallied around St. David and St. Cadoc. Many were North Britons driven from their homeland like Kentigern, the exiled bishop of Glasgow. Gildas was one of them, his pen breathing dragon's fire. In monasteries all along the south coast of Wales they enlisted and trained men brave enough and disciplined enough to lead the country out of its disaster.

One of the young men who trained with Kentigern was Asaph, a member of the royal house of Gwynedd in north Wales. About 560 AD Asaph was offered a grant of land on the Elwy river as a place to build a monastery near the north Welsh coast.

"St. Kentigern had set his mind on building a monastery"† reads a twelfth century text, "in which the scattered sons of God might come together like bees, from east and west, from north and south.

"After prayers, they set manfully about their work; some cleared and levelled land, others built foundations, carried timber, erected with skill a church of planed woodwork after the British fashion". They enclosed it all in a *llan* or rampart and called it Llanelwy. The tributary river that joins the Elwy here is still called the Clwyd (Clyde) and its valley Strathclwyd. This can scarcely be accidental, though there seems to be no record of when the names were given.

Not surprisingly the "Island Dragon", the ex-monk King Maelgwn of Gwynedd, was not at all pleased to find

The Bay of the Curragh at the south end of Iona where Colum-cille and his "Island Soldiers" landed in 563.

View from Tor Abb, site of Columcille's cell at Iona. The flat rock may be his writing table. Below is the monastery well, St. Martin's Cross and the Isle of Mull across the strait.

a monastery rising only a dozen miles from his capital at Degannwy and he was very hostile. Kentigern somehow overcame his enmity, won his friendship and brought him back to the Christian cause.

Poor Maelgwn died of bubonic plague, probably in 563 AD when a second great epidemic swept across Britain. A last glimpse shows him demented with fear of the unseen killer, vainly barricading himself in his fortress.

In his "Life of St. Mungo or Kentigern" the Reverend Alexander Gits wrote, "St. Columba of Iona was an Irish prince and a friend of kings. He used his influence to unite the Christian leaders and brought Rhydderch of Strath-clyde and Maelgwn of north Wales into alliance."

It will be recalled that King Rhydderch Hael of Strath-clyde, leader of the Roman Party, had been driven into exile when the pagan Native Party triumphed after Arthur's defeat and death. The King had fled to his mother's kin in Ireland about the same time that his friend Bishop Kenti-gern escaped to south Wales. In Ireland Rhydderch and Columcille must surely have met and made common cause during the perilous years before the battle of Culdremne.

Now the tide of events had turned and was flowing strongly for the Christian cause so that the separate labours of Columcille and Kentigern began to merge together. The changed outlook of Brude macMaelchon of the Picts, due to Columcille's friendship, must have roused special interest in Gwynedd if Maelgwn was indeed Brude's father. The renewed support of the Church by Maelgwn due to Kentigern's friendship, helped to end the isolation of the Christians in Dalriada.

Rhydderch, the Christian champion, came back from exile to raise in Strathclyde the Green Standard and rally the remnant of the Roman Party among the *Gwyr y Gogledd* men of the North. Urien of Cumbria, "the Golden King", sprang to arms and led his Cumbrians to join him. Maelgwn had died but his son Rhun reigned as Island Dragon in his stead and the Christian alliance was stronger still. He sent the Welshmen, marching behind their Red Dragon, to reinforce Rhydderch's army. The Cross was in the field.

Their pagan opponents were commanded by Gwendolew and his brother Elifer, leaders of the Native Party. The Arch Druid Merlin was with their army, a poet who had won fame at the court of Cumbria but who now employed all his arts to rouse the pagan army to battle pitch.

The collision between the two armies came in 573 AD at Ardderyd on the river Esk, eight miles north of Carlisle. King Rhydderch's troops won a complete victory, shattering the Druidic army. It marked the end for the Native Party. Gwendolew was killed. Legend tells that the disaster so unhinged Merlin's wits that he ended his days as a wild man of the woods in the Forest of Ettrick.

Thirty-six years had passed since Arthur had gone down in defeat at Camlann, years in which the Christian faith had come close to annihilation among the Britons and the Gaels. But at Culdremne the defeat had been redeemed and at Ardderyd it had been converted into victory.

Back on his throne of Strathclyde, the victorious Rhydderch found that "the Christian religion was almost completely destroyed in his kingdom", to quote Jocelyn. "He sent messengers to St. Kentigern to recall him to his first See."

There were about nine hundred monks serving at Llanelwy when the King's message came and six hundred and sixty-five of them promptly volunteered to got with Bishop Kentigern to tackle the re-conversion of northern Britain. At a solemn commissioning in the Abbey, Asaph was consecrated Bishop and installed as the new Abbot. Then the gallant six hundred volunteers followed Kentigern out of the north door because he was going forth to combat the northern enemy. Thereafter that door was never opened except on St. Asaph's day. In Norman times the name of the Abbey was changed to St. Asaph's but to the Welsh it is still known by its first title *Eglwys Gadeiriol Llanelwy*.

At Hoddam near Dumfries, King Rhydderch had a royal castle and here the two old friends met. After a quarter of a century in exile they were home and together again. They celebrated with a great thanksgiving festival during which Rhydderch knelt before the Bishop and placed his realm into God's hands.

For eight years Bishop Kentigern — now we must call him St. Mungo — had his base at Hoddam, rebuilding and vitalising the Church in Cumbria. Then at last in 581 after 35 years away, St. Mungo returned to his "beloved congregation". *Eglais chu* — Glasgow.

Ten years after Columcille landed in the besieged beach-head of Dalriada the outlook was dramatically transformed. To the east of Iona the land was ruled by Columcille's *amn chara* Brude, High King of the Picts. To the south the Christian champions Rhydderch and Urien

governed Strathclyde and Cumbria, advised by Bishop
Mungo of Glasgow. Gwynedd was led by Rhun, aided by
Bishop Asaph. Further south the work of the Welsh saints
went powerfully forward in south Wales, Cornwall and
Brittany. The Church militant and monastic was on the
march from the Orkneys to Brittany. All the reclaimed
lands lay open to the Irish "saints and scholars" pouring
from the colleges of Bangor, Clonmacnois, Derry, Clonfert, Aran and Glendalough.

For the Britons and Gaels the great War of Faiths had
been won. They had chosen Christ and from that date
onward that decision, though at times seriously threatened, has never been reversed.

King Conall of the Dalriad Scots died in 575 AD. He deserves honourable mention in the annals of the nation because it was his appeal for help that brought Columcille to Iona and set in motion such far-ranging impulses.

This was only one year after the victory of Ardderyd, Britain was still in a disturbed state and Dalriada remained the linchpin of the Christian alliance. Therefore the choice of a successor to Conall was of more than local significance.

Under the Gaelic Law of Tanistry the first claims to the inheritance lay with Eoghan and Aidan, sons of King Gabhran who had fallen fighting the Picts in 559 AD. Kingship was "hereditary as to the family" and his sons were the seniors of all who were *rigdomna* in the Royal Family. But Kingship was also "elective as to the individual". It was the duty of the Scots nobles to choose which of the two sons was "the most noble, experienced, wise and best able to lead in battle."

Little is known of Eoghan except that he was a warm friend of Columcille who was inclined to favour his claim. His half-brother Aidan was the son of Lleian, a daughter of the saintly King Brychan of Strathclyde, and through her he was a nephew of Urien of Cumbria. By right of his mother he was a sub-king of Manaan, the present Stirlingshire, and for some years he had been governing that province of the Britons. His wife, it is believed, was a grand-daughter of Brude macMaelchon of the Picts. He was a leader of the Roman Party and had fought with distinction at Ardderyd under the command of Rhydderch.†

Aidan therefore had royal blood-ties with the Britons and Picts, experience in government and military distinction.

Aidan's hero and model was Arthur and he named his eldest son after him. His life aim was to fulfill Arthur's dream of uniting the Christian princes and driving out the heathen invaders.

As the religious leader of the Dalriad Scots, Columcille had been premier adviser to the late King Conall. Among Gaelic people it was a role always filled by the arch druid or religious leader. When a King died it was his legal duty to supervise the choice of a successor. Furthermore by ancient custom the religious leader was required to seek in a dream or a trance the identity of the true Heir. A majority vote by mere mortals was not considered to be a sufficient mandate to confirm a King in so sacred an office; divine proof was also needed.

Columcille, who sought God's will in every decision, doubtless sought the Almighty's will in the choice of a successor. To meditate on the question he withdrew to the remote and rocky isle of Hinba, a place where the Brethren went who wished for a time of strict meditation. His uncle Ernan was the Prior of the island and it was here that his own beloved mother Eithne had died and been buried.

Columcille had a Bible-based trust in divine direction being given in dreams: had not the Prophets and Apostles been so guided? And as a Gael belief in dreams was in his blood. He said that "three times in a trance of the mind" he was commanded to choose Aidan and, in spite of his friendship with Eoghan, he obeyed.

In one historical book Columcille's choice was denounced as "strong-handed intervention in politics — and that, being sensible of the illegality of his action, he sought to invest it with religious sanction by inventing the story of the trance."

Such a view must result from failure to understand the Law of Tanistry but reference to a Lineage Chart of the Dalriad Kings shows how strictly legal was the succession of Gabhran's sons. Of the two candidates, the nobles elected Aidan because they judged him better qualified, a choice confirmed by divine revelation. This is an almost perfect working model of the Tanist Law. And Aidan proved to be the best King Dalriada ever had.

To charge that Columcille invented the trance is to call him a cheat and liar in the most sacred sphere of his Faith. Only a priest madly craving political power would sink to such a sin. But if Columcille had been politically ambitious, would he have been content to live and work in a minor country like Dalriada? Twice, we are told, he refused the sceptre of Ireland, the second time probably in 572 when his claim to it was very strong. And in those days priests did become kings and kings became bishops and "separation of Church and State" was a concept of the far future.

Is it credible that a man who refused the title of *Ard Ri* could be so politically self-seeking that he would perjure his soul? And for what purpose?

Aidan was ordained King of Scots in 574 by Columcille at Iona by the laying on of hands, the first monarch in British history to receive Christian consecration.

There is a prayer preserved in the Leofric Missal believed to have been used at the ordination of King Aidan. "O Lord, Who from everlasting governs the Kingdom of Kings, bless this ruling prince that he may hold the sceptre of salvation. Grant him Your inspiration to rule his people in peace. May he be protected by Your shield ever to remain a conqueror without a combat. May the Nation keep faith with him. May the nobles love charity and may he hold from You a firm seat of government."

Why was this religious act so essential? The authority of a Gaelic king was rooted in religion. He was the reincarnation of the tribal god-ancestor: in the case of the Dalriad Scots this was Eochaid-the-Horseman-of-Heaven, the spirit of the sun. Obviously the authority of a Christian King could not derive from a sun-god. Facing this problem, Columcille realised that King Aidan must be seen by his people to hold his authority in trust from God Himself; hence the need for the King's ordination.

"That day the real foundation of the Scottish monarchy was laid" wrote Bishop Reeves, and today Queen Elizabeth, Aidan's heir by right of descent, sits upon the throne of Great Britain, holding her dominion "by Grace of God."

In his person Aidan combined all the racial strands which were to form the future nation. His father was a Scot, which still meant an Irishman. His mother was a Briton and her mother had been a Saxon princess. Aidan's wife was a Pict and so he drew together in himself the promise of unity to come.

The new King had at once to face a threat to his realm which was developing from Ireland. In 572 AD an aggressive warrior Baetan macCairell became king of Ulidia in

The Great War

KINGS OF THE DALRIAD SCOTS

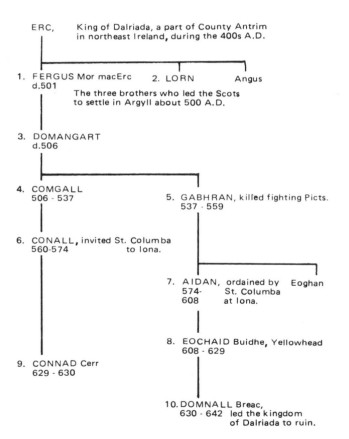

ERC,   King of Dalriada, a part of County Antrim
        in northeast Ireland, during the 400s A.D.

1. FERGUS Mor macErc   2. LORN   Angus
   d.501
                The three brothers who led the Scots
                to settle in Argyll about 500 A.D.

3. DOMANGART
   d.506

4. COMGALL
   506 - 537   5. GABHRAN, killed fighting Picts.
                         537 - 559

6. CONALL, invited St. Columba
   560-574   to Iona.

                  7. AIDAN, ordained by   Eoghan
                     574-   St. Columba
                     608   at Iona.

                  8. EOCHAID Buidhe, Yellowhead
                     608 - 629

9. CONNAD Cerr
   629 - 630

                 10. DOMNALL Breac,
                     630 - 642 led the kingdom
                                of Dalriada to ruin.

Ulster and launched an expansionist policy. The old
lands belonging to Dalriada back in Ireland (in County
Antrim) were still vassals to the King of Ulidia and Baetan
used this fact to force King Aidan to make submission to
him at Island Magee in Ulster and to yield up hostages. It
is not clear if submission was made only for the Irish lands
or for Scottish Dalriada as well. There had been a battle at
Delgon in Argyll where Duncan, son of King Conall, was
killed. This may have been part of the pressure Baetan put
on the Scots to force them to submit. The real prize that
Baetan was after was the Dalriad fleet, the largest and best
in the narrow seas, able to muster 70 galleys. With such a
naval force he dreamed of conquering the Isle of Man and
colonizing Galloway.†

Aidan and the Scots were in a perilous position. If they
resisted Baetan's demands, he would seize the Irish lands
of Dalriada. Yet it would be total disaster to yield up the
fleet. Because Aidan was their kinsman through his
mother and his wife, both the Britons and the Picts treated
the Scots of Dalriada as friends. But if the Scots' powerful
fleet fell into the hands of an aggressive Irish overlord,
neither Picts nor Britons would tolerate this immigrant
colony on their coast and would swiftly wipe it out.

This was the dilemma which faced King Aidan and the
Abbot of Iona and brought about their journey in 575 AD
to attend the Convention of Druim Ceatt in Ireland.

The bull of Burghead.

Chapter twenty-one

Both Aidan and Columcille attended the Convetion of Druim Ceatt which was held near Derry. It was initiated, Adomnan recorded, by Aed macAinmire, *Ard Ri* of Ireland, in 575 AD and brought together the kings and leading clergy to deal with two main issues: one, the relationship of the Scots of Dalriada to the Irish motherland; two, the sentence of exile that King Aed had passed upon the Order of the *Filidh*.

But this raises a problem. Records show that Aed macAinmire did not become *Ard Ri* until 586 AD. At the time of the Convention the *Ard Ri* was Baetan macNinnedo, Aed's cousin. Aed macAinmire was the provincial king of Ailech, and the Northern Ui Neill, though he was already the pre-eminent power in the land. Gearoid Mac-Niocaill has explained what probably was the real situation. "A tightening of Baetan macCairell's control over Dalriada was of military importance because of the fleet, and it represented a threat for the Northern Ui Neill . . . In substance the Druim Ceatt Convention was an agreement between Aed macAinmire and Aidan that the fleet of Dalriada should be regarded as an appurtenance of his Scottish lands, with the consequence that Baetan macCairell of Ulidia would have no claim on it in wartime."†

Columcille's diplomacy with the Picts had saved the existence of the Dalriad Scots and Iona had grown up in their midst to be the main training base for missionaries going out to Christianize the Picts. He was not prepared to see that base endangered by the ambitions of a warlord. There can be no doubt that he put King Aidan in touch with Aed macAinmire of Ailech, his own cousin who had given him the land for his first monastery at Derry.

Sailing from Iona to Ireland to attend the Convention, Columcille's ship was caught in a bad storm while navigating the treacherous Gulf of Corryvrechan between Scarba and Jura.

As the curragh began to ship water he bailed furiously but the sailors yelled at him, "What you're doing doesn't help. You ought to be praying." He followed their advice, the weather moderated and they came through safely.

It was probably on this occasion that St. Kenneth, who was preparing dinner in the refectory of his Abbey at Achabo in Leinster, "heard a warning in the inner ear of the heart" that his friend's ship was in danger. Racing from the dining hall, one shoe on, one shoe off, he shouted, "We can't have dinner now. Columcille's in danger!" and gathered all the Brethren in the chapel to pray. The story shows what a close, life-long comradeship bound together the Clonard men and made them such an effective force.

> "Forty priests were their number,
> Twenty Bishops noble and worthy,
> For singing Psalms — a blameless practice —
> Fifty Deacons, thirty Students."

With this retinue drawn from Derry, Durrow, Iona, Kells and his other foundations, the Abbot arrived to meet the Kings at Druim Ceatt. The Convention was held upon a ridge fifteen miles east of Derry now called Mullagh Hill, near Limavady. It was shaped rather like a whale and the words Druim Ceatt mean the whale's back. Baetan macCairell of Ulidia did not attend and perhaps he was not invited. Very wisely the Kings called upon the famous judge *Olave Brieve* Colman macComgellan to adjudicate the new legal relationship between the Dalriad Scots and the men of Ireland.

Dalriada as a vassal had paid to the Ulidian overlord *cain*, a yearly tax of 7 shields, 7 steeds, 7 hounds, 7 bondsmen; they had rendered *cobach*, military service; *fecht*, joining in expeditions; and *slogad*, hosting or general mobilisation.

Colman's judgement was: "Dalriada's *fecht* and *slogad* with the men of Ireland for ever. Their *cain* and *cobach* with the men of Alban and their sea service with Alban alone."†

Aidan and his Scots now became in fact an independent kingdom, free from taxes and from the duty of military or naval service. The rather vague commitment to "hosting with the men of Ireland for ever" was probably put in as a face-saving item so that Baetan could not accuse Aidan of repudiating the submission he had made at Island Magee.

Baetan macCairell had lost his gamble to get his hands on the Dalriad fleet. He dared not even invade Irish Dalriada in revenge because it would bring down upon him the might of the Ui Neill. All he was strong enough to do was seize the Isle of Man and hold it for a few years.

Adomnan said that Columcille pleaded with King Aed to release the hostage Scannlan, son of the king of Ossary, who was being ill-treated to force the payment of tribute. However, this incident must belong to a later date after Aed became *Ard Ri*. It shows how the Church constantly battled for the humane treatment of prisoners.

The major crisis facing King Aed at Druim Ceatt concerned the Order of *Filidh*. These privileged intellectuals

had steadily increased in numbers. Exploiting their right
of *coinmed* — free food and lodging — they had developed
into an idle, satirical, argumentative host of free-loaders
badgering and beggaring the working population. In
their arrogance *Olave Filidh* were even demanding an
escort of thirty attendants, equal to royalty.

The people were up in revolt against them and the King
had angrily issued an edict banishing the entire Order
from his lands.

The Christians suffered much from the satires and hostility of the largely druidic *Filidh*. Yet Columcille himself
had been educated in their disciplines and highly prized
the ancient poetic learning. He foresaw what a disaster it
would be for the land if it lost its whole learned class;
lawyers, historians, poets. He saw too that here was a
wealth of ability that could be recruited for the work of the
monasteries. So he offered to arbitrate.

King Aed withdrew the edict of banishment. *Olave Filidh*
contented themselves with a noble's escort of twenty-four.
The *Order of Filidh* gave up its right of *coinmed,* to the
jubilation of the farmers. In compensation all *Filidh* were
given land on which to earn their own living.

The chief bard of Ireland, blind Dallan Forgaill, was so
delighted with this sane settlement that he wrote a majestic
eulogy called *Amhra* in honour of Columcille, the first
poem ever written down in Gaelic. Twelve hundred *Filidh*
sang it to him and few things in his life gave him greater
pleasure. But he asked them not to sing it again till after he
was dead.

Many talented *Filidh* were attracted to the work of the
monasteries where they learned to use their gifts to serve

rather than exploit the people. Thus the orally preserved lore of countless centuries mingled with the written Latin scholarship, both enriching the other, and the steam of Celtic culture flowed on in unbroken continuity through the Church. In many lands the pre-Christian culture was over-laid and lost but thanks to the wise provisions of Druim Ceatt the Celtic lore and traditions were written down and survive to this day in Ireland.

Columcille's way

S. COLUMBA

From a drawing in a ninth century MS of Adomnan's life of St. Columba at Stiftsbibliotek, St. Gallen, Switzerland.

In Adomnan's book Columcille does not expound doctrine nor often preach sermons. He lived what he believed and it is his actions that speak. Perhaps that is fortunate because words change their meaning over the centuries but actions do not. We learn about Columcille's motives, beliefs, and teaching by following his journies and seeing him in action throughout Ireland and Scotland, but especially by watching the way he lived at Iona. That was Columcille's way.

When the Druim Ceatt Convention ended Columcille walked over the hills to Coleraine with his close friend Comgall of Bangor. He had been invited by Bishop Conall of Coleraine and a welcoming crowd awaited him at the church, where the courtyard was filled with gifts collected by the local people. Such support was very acceptable for the upkeep of his monastic houses. The monks never had much of a surplus as they gave to the poor any excess they had. The Abbot passed from gift to gift blessing it and the giver.

But at one offering he stopped short. "I can touch nothing of this gift from a clever but greedy man until he repents of his avarice." he declared. Word of his outburst quickly reached the donor. He was Columb, son of King Aed and the Abbot's own namesake. Generosity was expected of a prince of the Gaels and lack of it in his own kinsman angered Columcille's royal blood. But beyond this, he prized the young man more highly than he prized his gift.

"Columb, conscience-stricken, ran to him" narrated Adomnan, "and kneeling, promised to mend his ways and practice generosity. From that hour he was cured of the vice of meanness."

Columcille had a way of drawing out the best in youngsters. When visiting the monastery at Raphoe in Donegal he found the monks in trouble. It was time to put in the spring seed but their only ploughshare was broken and there was no blacksmith in the region to repair it. There was a boy at Raphoe just at the age when youngsters know everything to the annoyance of their elders. He begged the Abbot to let him try to repair it. Columcille was not thinking about the ploughshare or the crop, but about the boy. He took both his hands in his own, blessed them for the service of God and told him to get to work. He succeeded in mending the ploughshare and grew up to be a blacksmith renowned for the beauty of his workmanship.

An invitation came for Columcille to visit Clonmacnois, founded by his old friend Ciaran the carpenter's son. Ciaran was long dead but his foundation had grown into a famous seat of learning. To welcome Columcille, Abbot Alither brought out the whole community onto the green banks of the Shannon "greeting him as if he were an angel of God." In the throng was a scruffy, mischievous lad who was the despair of his teachers. Boy-like he wormed through the crush until he was close enough to tweak a thread from the great man's cowl. Cheek is often close to hero worship.

Columcille reached back, caught the lad by the neck and pulled him round in front. Some of the elders said crossly, "Send him away. He's a nuisance." "Let him alone" ordered the Abbot and then to the boy he said: "Put out your tongue, son." When he obeyed Columcille marked it with the Saving Sign. Turning to the scowling Seniors, he said, "You don't think much of this young fellow, do you? But he will become a distinguished man in your community, famous for his eloquence." The boy became Ernan macCrasene, a preacher known throughout Ireland.

It may have been soon after Druim Ceatt that Columcille had a strangely moving meeting with an old antagonist. Tradition recounted that he was staying at Kells when he received an impelling thought to set out on the road to Tara. After some miles he overtook another traveller, an old man walking slowly. He was Bec macDe, the Arch Druid who had been adviser to *Ard Ri* Diarmit during the stormy years before the fall of Tara. For all that, he was a fine man and Abbot and Druid respected each other. As they walked towards Tara together Columcille asked, "Has it been revealed to you how long you have to live?" Bec answered, "Yes, I have seven years to live." "A Man can do much good in seven years", replied Columcille. Some distance further on Bec declared, "What I told you is not true. I have seven weeks to live." "A man can do much good in seven weeks" said Columcille.

They walked on in silence for some time, then suddenly Bec macDe wept, "Never in my life have I lied about a revelation until now. But I have lied to you. I know that I have only seven hours to live." Columcille took his arm. "Then let us spend them together."

On the ramparts of abandoned Tara they sat together talking of the past and the future. No other man after macDe would ever again celebrate the *Feis* here. At last the sun went down and, as was fitting, the Arch Druid passed peacefully away in the arms of the priest.

After Tara had been abandoned in 563 AD the title of *Ard Ri* lost much of its significance. With no Druidic rites to celebrate, the office of a sacral King seemed purposeless. Following Diarmit's death the title was held from 566 to 569 by Ainmire, one of the victorious commanders of the battle of Culdremne.

His first act had been to invite St. Gildas to come from Wales to consolidate the recovery of the Church in Ireland.

But the real political power passed away from Tara to the Northern Ui Neill kings of Ailech. Not until Aed macAinmire became *Ard Ri* in 586 AD did something of its old majesty return.

There is some evidence in the records to suggest that Columcille may have had some part in its revival. His ordination of Aidan as King of Scots was the result of deep thought about the role of kingship in a Christian state and naturally his ideas were influenced by the Biblical concept of "the Lord's Anointed". There is an echo of this idea in his warning to prince Aed Slaine, Diarmit's son. "Avoid the sin of fratricide" he told him, "or you will lose the kingdom which God has foreordained for you."

In Ireland Columcille founded the monasteries of Derry, Kells, Durrow, Lambay, Swords, Drumcliff, Glen-columcille, Tory Island and at least thirty more. In Dal-riada of the Scots he founded Iona, Hinba, Tiree and Loch Awe. In Alban in cooperation with his nephew Drostan, he founded Aberdour and Deer. Bede wrote that all the monasteries in the land of the Picts were Columban but he is not likely to have founded them himself. Dr. Lucy Menzies gave a list of 53 churches in Scotland associated with his name and he is reputed to have built 300 churches and supplied each with a Gospel or Psalter from his own pen. Whatever the precise figures, it was a formidable organizational work.

Organizer, educator, scribe, philosopher, he was all these. In every task he retained the eager curiosity and enthusiasm of a boy. He loved nature, as all Gaels do, and had learnt from the *Filidh* the habits of birds, fish and animals, the growth of plants and the interplay of climate. He knew something of astral navigation and he studied the cycles of the tides. He built steps on a stream to help salmon ascend to spawn and experimented with bee culture and grafting fruit trees. In this he was a forerunner of the monks of the Middle Ages who pioneered new methods of farming.

He was one of the finest scholars of his age, yet from youth he had set his mind to learn a wisdom that went beyond mere knowledge. A monk at Iona remembered that "he prayed a hundred times a day", which simply meant that prayer was integral to his whole thought process. He prayed while he thought and he thought while he prayed. His mind was brilliant: prayer made it inspired.

We see him in Adomnan's narrative, a tall, handsome, happy man, an all-weather sailor with smiling eyes and the flash of Gaelic wit on his tongue, "the kind Columcille, beloved of all because joy beamed on his face, revealing the gladness of his soul." A man of dynamic energy, "who never could spend an hour without study, writing or other holy work."

Above all he was engrossed in caring for people. His method of remaking the world, of changing the system, was to make bad men good and good men better. This was the continuous outcome of his work wherever he went. The impossible became possible when the hearts of men were changed.

Forty miles north of Iona was the island of Eigg where his friend St. Donnen founded a monastery. On one of his visits to Eigg Columcille noticed that two of the young monks were rivals, vying to be called the best preacher. One was tall and the other short, so he asked them both to lift their arms up as high as they could. "One of you is a little taller," he observed, "but neither of you can reach that cloud up there. Pray for each other and you'll reach higher than the clouds." They got the point. The story adds, "Their prayers which used to stick in the thatch, now mounted like sparks. They became friends and made brothers of the folk who dwelt around."

Columcille could not have cured their rivalry if he himself had been suffering from the same malady. Yet some writers have fancied that he was a rival of St. Moluag "the gleaming light of Lismore." They cite as proof that both of them founded monastic houses on the island of Tiree. Surely this points to cooperation rather than competition. Tiree, which means the land of corn, was the granary for the Hebrides and the monasteries of Bangor, Lismore and Iona maintained monastic farms on the island. Had there been rivalry between the missionary saints their efforts would have "stuck in the thatch" and they would have been long since forgotten.

Warmhearted and understanding with the repentant, the Abbot of Iona could be terrible when he encountered deliberate sin. Hearing that the priest of Trevet was a bad-living man, he decided to attend Mass at his church. As the Bread and Wine were being consecrated, he rose and his voice rang out, "Now we see a marvel; the clean and the unclean together!" The Priest was shocked out of his hypocrisy and falling on his face, confessed the whole sordid business. This drastic soul-surgery was successful and the man lived to become a worthy priest.

The ships that constantly sailed between Iona and Ireland followed the coastal route through the Sound of Jura and along the coast of Kintyre and then across a dozen miles of open sea to Ireland. This stretch was dangerous whenever the Atlantic swells met a rip tide surging up the North Channel. Pilots living on Rathlin island just off the Antrim coast made their living guiding ships through these perilous waters.

Lugne Tudicla was a pilot who came to see Columcille once when he was staying on Rathlin. The poor fellow was in despair. He was an unusually ugly man and his wife had flatly refused to share his bed. Columcille talked to the wife, explaining that she was rejecting her own flesh as they had been "made one flesh" in holy matrimony. "Father, I will do anything you tell me," cried the unhappy woman, "I'll even become a nun. But I will *not* live with that man!"

Hill of Druim Ceatt, scene of Convention in 575 AD.
Photo: Canon G.W.A. Knowles, Limavady.

Columcille put forward a proposal. "There are three of us — husband, wife and me. Let us all fast and pray about the matter for twenty-four hours." They agreed.

In the morning the wife came to the Abbot radiant. "Father, I shall not have to be a nun," said she, "I don't know how it happened. Yesterday I hated that man. I woke this morning and I am in love with him!" Adomnan concluded. "From that day till death the wife's affections were set in love for her husband."

On one of his journies among the Picts he travelled up the Great Glen and was entertained by a Pict in Glen Urquart, not far from Inverness. He had to talk to them through an interpreter but the whole household believed, and the father, mother, children and the servants were all baptised.

The Abbot resumed his journey but had not gone far when word reached him that the Pict's son had been taken ill and died. He hurried back to the Glen and found the stricken family preparing for the funeral, while all around the house a crowd of Druids shouted taunts at them. "Don't doubt God's power", he told the parents and asked the father to take him to the room where the boy was lying. He went in alone and prayed. At last he commanded, "In the Name of the Lord Jesus Christ, stand up." The boy opened his eyes and Columcille, steadying him on his feet, led him out alive to his parents.

"Let this miracle of power", wrote Adomnan, "be attributed to Columba, in common with Elijah." Critics have pointed out that the words and deeds of this event are so like the Bible story of Elijah raising the widow's son that Adomnan simply copied it. However, Columcille also knew the story of Elijah and it may well have influenced his words and acts.

Adomnan was in a good position to ascertain the facts. In his day there was a Columban monastery in Glen Urquart which was under the jurisdiction of the Abbot of Iona. Doubtless some of the grandchildren of the Pict family would still be alive and some may even have heard the story at first hand. It seems certain that Adomnan believed the story was true and just as certain that the Picts of Glen Urquart believed it. The point that Adomnan was making in his book was, not that Columcille was a great man, but that God is a great God, the same yesterday, today and all the days to come.

Whether the problem which faced Columcille was a dead soul, a dead heart or a dead body, he applied the same cure — the Power of God. And the result was the same — a miracle of new life.

Everything at Iona came and went by sea, news, supplies, visitors, so the port was a focus of ceaseless activity. From his cell on top of the rocky hillock of Tor Abb Columcille looked down on the port, watched the ships moving in the strait and kept a knowing eye on shifts of wind and weather.

> "At the mouth of the day
> The hour of birds,
> Stood Columba
> On the great white strand.
> O King of storms,
> From far away
> Home sail the boat."

Not much that went on around the island escaped the Abbot's notice. Some of his men had built a small lagoon on the islet of Soay, two miles south of Iona, where they raised baby seals for oil, meat and hides. When the seals began to disappear he had a shrewd idea where they were going. On the island of Colonsay lived Erc-the-Druid's-Son, a poacher who had developed a habit of raiding the monks' lagoon. One day the Abbot sent two muscular young clerics Lugbe and Silnan to catch him while he was hiding under his boat, waiting for dusk. They returned dragging a very frightened thief. On such an occasion Columcille was an awe-inspiring figure.

"Why do you repeatedly steal other people's property and break God's law?" he demanded. "When you are in want, why don't you come to us and ask? We shall see that you get what you need." Thereupon he set the poacher free, ordering that a sheep be killed and given to him so that he would not return home empty-handed.

Some years later news came that Erc-the-Druid's-son was dying and Columcille sent over the Colonsay a lamb and six measures of meal. The gift arrived in time to provide a fitting funeral feast, such an important rite among the Gaels.

A mile across the straits east of Iona was little *Eilean nam Ban* — woman's island. Woven around its name grew up an odd myth that Columcille banned women and even female animals from Iona. Adomnan had not heard the tale because he wrote about the cow pasture and the white pony which carried the milk pails. There were married men among the Iona rowers and among "the islanders, its inhabitants" blessed by Columcille on the last day of his life. Of course women did not enter the monastic buildings any more than men entered nunneries. But Columcille's mother, it seems, lived and died on Hinba, the most privileged retreat of the Iona community, and it is unlikely that she was the only woman there.

The reason Eilean nam Ban got its name is probably due to the fact that there is no good anchorage on Iona's east shore. Anchors drag and any ship too large to be beached must sail across the Sound to Eilean nam Ban where in the channel between the island and Mull they find good anchorage and a sheltered berth. The fishermen and crews of trade ships who sailed out of this anchorage made their homes on the island. When the men were away at sea and only their wives at home it must indeed have seemed like an island of women.

Sympathy and unfailing courtesy marked Columcille's

conduct with women. The callous murder of an unknown girl, witnessed while he was a deacon, ignited a lifelong passion to establish Church sanctuary for fugitives. On his embassy to the High King of the Picts, while engaged in weighty affairs of state, he was not too preoccupied to use his influence to free a slave girl. And this in an age when a *cumhall* — the price of a slave girl — was still a standard unit of barter.

There is a charming story of the Abbot on Iona dropping his pen and running from his writing hut to the church when he had a presentiment that a girl cousin in Ireland was undergoing a painful delivery. "Jesus, born of Mary, help the sufferer . . .", the prayer he composed at the time, has comforted many women since then.

A nun named Maugin at Clochar in Ireland suffered great pain from a broken hip, often a fatal injury in those days. From Iona he sent one of his monks to treat her with a salve he had compounded, assuring her of the Brethren's prayers, and writing on the lid of the medicine box his prophecy that she would live another twenty years. In that way he treated the body, mind and spirit of his patient.

Healing played a large part in his work. Trained in the medical art of the *Filidh*, he used his skill to cure diseases. For instance, the sister of the monk Colcu suffered from inflamed eyes which he treated with rock salt. But always through prayer he linked his patients with the regenerative power of God so that "many people, believing, regained full health."

Even a storm-blown crane received medical care on Iona. Most Gaels would have nothing to do with this bird of ill omen but when the Abbot heard that one had fallen exhausted on the beach he assigned a Brother to feed and care for it for three days — the statutory hospitality offered to a stranger — and then release it. The revived bird rose in the air, circled the island and then winged away towards Ireland.

One day the Abbot spotted a whale cruising in the straits between Iona and Tiree, where they still are occasionally seen. Some of the rowers were taking cargo across to Tiree that day and the Abbot cautioned them to hug the coast of Mull as long as they could so as to have the shortest passage across the open sea. But this would double the 30-mile voyage, so the sailors ignored the warning. When they were well out from the shore suddenly the whale breached alongside, nearly swamping the curragh, and some very scared seamen rowed for their lives towards Mull.

The same day Prior Baithen, who ran the monastery farm on Tiree, planned to return there but the Abbot tried to dissuade him because of the whale. "The beast and I are both in God's power" rejoined Baithen and set sail. When the whale surfaced close to his ship, Baithen stood up in the bows and blessed him.

"On a day of crashing storms and high waves at Iona the Abbot called to his people, 'quickly prepare the Guest House. A holy man will be here this evening.'" As Adomnan tells it, the Brothers protested that no one could cross to the island in such a storm. Nevertheless that evening Kenneth of Achabo sailed into port. His sailors reported that they had seen the storm on the horizon but on the course they were sailing they had enjoyed excellent weather.

Nowhere does Adomnan imply that Columcille altered the weather or tried to control it in the manner of the Druids. But like Baithen and the whale, he believed that if he was in tune with the Creator of nature, he would be in tune with nature too, all part of the same unfolding plan.

His sea-going friend Cormac O'Lethan, who had evangelised the Orkneys, was returning to Ireland some time about 580 when a steady south-east gale drove his curraghs out into the Atlantic for fourteen days "till he seemed beyond the bounds of human experience." That day the sea seemed to boil around them, alive with swimming, stinging creatures the size of frogs, which clogged the oars and struck the hulls with such force as if they would break the leather sheathing of the boats.

An unnerving experience. Most likely the creatures were blue stinging jellyfish called "cyanoea capillata" which sometimes wash up on the coast of Florida in such numbers that the beaches are blue for miles.

On Iona Columcille sensed that his friend's little fleet was in trouble and he rallied the Island Soldiers to the church to pray for a homeward breeze. Two weeks later Cormac and his crews limped into port at Iona, weary but unhurt after a month out in mid-Atlantic. Later on Cormac became Prior of the monastery of Durrow.

An old friend Bishop Colman of Lagin, one of the Clonard men, sailed up to Iona to visit him and Baithen came over from Tiree to join them. For three leisured days they walked and talked of the struggles and victories of the past and of the opportunities that lay ahead. Then it was time for them to leave. Baithen needed to sail north-west to return to Tiree; Bishop Colman had to sail south-east on his return to Ireland. They put the problem to Colum-cille, how could they sail opposite courses on the same day?

"Baithen must sail at dawn and the Bishop must sail after the third hour (9 a.m.)" promptly answered the Abbot and the wind proved just right for both journeys. Weather-wise, he knew there would be an off-shore wind at dawn and a return wind as soon as the sun grew warm.

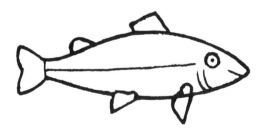

On the Roseisle symbol stone.

Penance was a natural idea to the Gael, like paying the *eric* blood fine to God. Anyone who was truly sorry for the wrongs he had done was eager to put them right in any way he could. Great numbers of penitents came to Iona in the hope of finding forgiveness. God's forgiveness was a free gift but it could not be cheap. Christ laid down His life to win it for mankind and the penitents knew that they must lay down their own old way of life to pay the blood fine.

The Brethren treated sin as a deadly epidemic disease which could not be tolerated in "a colony of Heaven". It was a serious matter and, when necessary, the Abbot dealt trenchantly with sin, as on one occasion when he reprimanded a gifted but idle young Brother in a voice so loud it was heard in Mull a mile away across the straits. It is not likely the Brother ever forgot it. But much as he hated sin, he loved the sinner and never dwelt on the faults of others.

Word came to the island that Fechna, a fine man but who had fallen into grave sin, was arriving by ship and the Abbot hurried to the beach to meet him. In utter despair the man fell on his knees sobbing. Columcille lifted him up saying, "Rise, my son. A broken and contrite heart God does not despise." He sent him off to Tiree where under the kindly discipline of Prior Baithen he worked out his penance and rebuilt his life.

Columcille's compassion for sinners sprang from a keen sense that he was a sinner himself. His foster-son and successor Baithen once had a dream in which he saw three thrones in Heaven; one was gold, one was silver and one was glass. Among the Gaels dreams were regarded with awe and Christians also felt they had religious meaning, so Baithen went to the Abbot and asked him to interpret the dream.

"Easy to say," replied Columcille. "The gold throne belongs to Ciaran the carpenter's son because of his honour and hospitality. The silver throne is yours, Baithen, because of your purity and devotion. The glass throne is mine because, although my devotion is fairly good, I am often brittle and worldly."

Honest about himself, he was realistic about others and was not easily fooled. He was not much impressed by gloomy, pious people. He said to the monk Colcu one day, "Is your mother truly religious?" "She is very devout and respected" answered Colcu. But Columcille sensed a lack of the joy which comes to God-freed people. "Go and ask her if she has ever confessed a grave sin she has hidden" he suggested.

Reluctantly Colcu put the question to his mother, who furiously denied it. Finally she broke down in tears and told her son about the private ghost which had haunted her for many years. She became a free and vital woman, able to help people around her.

On the island of Tiree one of the monastic houses was run by a certain Bishop Findchan who arrived back from Ireland one day bringing a convert who was notorious as "a very bloody man, a slayer of many". He was Aed Dubh macSuibne, Black Aed who in 565 had speared *Ard Rí* Diarmit to death at Banban's inn. Had Columcille ever craved revenge against Diarmit as some books claim, he might have welcomed and lionised Black Aed, the regicide. However, he discerned that Aed's conversion was more an act than a fact and he warned the Bishop that he would turn back again to his old evil ways. "But the Bishop's love for Aed was earthly", wrote Adomnan. He was proud of his prize convert and was blinded both to the needs and the motives of the man.

In spite of Columcille's vigorous protest, Findchan actually ordained Black Aed as a priest. But in 581 death removed the ambitious King Baetan macCairell of Ulidia and Black Aed saw his chance to succeed to that realm and he threw off the priest's cowl and departed from Tiree in haste. He managed to enforce his claim and ruled Ulidia for a few turbulent years, being slain at last by treachery in one of the endless, senseless clan feuds.

The story of Liban-of-the-Reed-Patch ended rather differently. The Abbot found a stranger one day sitting alone in a corner of the Guest House at Iona. He was a Connaught man, a fugitive from justice seeking the sanctuary of the Church. He had murdered a man and since neither he nor his family had been able to pay the *eric* fine, he had been put in chains to await execution. A rich man however paid the *eric* and won his reprieve on condition he serve as his bondsman for life. Grateful at first, his proud warrior spirit was soon galled by being a slave and he ran away.

The Abbot talked the matter over with him and they decided that as penance he should work for seven years on Tiree. "Then come to me and we will talk again," said Columcille.

For a Gaelic warrior discipline was almost unknown; he did what he wanted when he wanted and, apart from hunting, rarely did any work. So for the Connaughtman the ordered life of the monastery farm was a wholly new way of living, regulated by the church bell ringing for the services. Doubtless some of his colleagues on the farm were also criminals yet they were in no sense prisoners. To the monks penance was not punishment but medicine. The status of the penitent was respected because it had bene accepted voluntarily. His service was dedicated to God and he was regarded as an Island Soldier just as much as the Abbot himself.

The Connaughtman was put in charge of the reed patch and by the time seven years had passed he had grown into a fine, firm Christian character. He returned to Iona and talked again with the Abbot. His own conviction was that he must go back to Ireland and surrender himself to his master. The Abbot gave him a valuable ivory-handled sword to take as a peace offering.

When he arrived back at his master's house and told his tale, the master's wife declared, "If the holy Abbot of Iona has set him free, who are we to enslave him again? Columcille's blessing will profit us much more." In the ancient rite of manumission his master unloosed the captive's belt and set him at liberty.

But his brothers complained, "We have supported our old parents all the years you were away." At once he accepted the responsibility and began to take care of his mother and father. But after a year, when his father died, his youngest brother said, "Let me take care of mother so that you can return to God's work at Iona."

So, all debts discharged, he sailed back to receive a joyful welcome at Iona. In the church before all the

Brethren he took his vows as a monk and during his ordination, Columcille said, "From now on let your name be 'Liban' — because you are free."

Allies

Pope Gregory's marble table in St. Andrew's monastery, Rome.

LET GLASGOW   THE WORD

FLOURISH BY PREACHING

Arms of the city of Glasgow showing bell given by Pope Gregory to St. Mungo. The fish and ring is St. Mungo's symbol.

Chapter twenty-six

Death came to Brude macMaelchon, High King of the Picts, in 584 AD. For twenty years he had been Columcille's *amn-chara,* soul friend. He had been a true friend and peace and security had been his gift to Iona. Adomnan shows no instance of warfare between Pict and Scot while he lived. He left his kingdom adorned with monasteries where Picts learned to become "saints and scholars" under the tutoring of the monks from Lismore and Iona. He was succeeded as High King by Gartnaidh macDomelch, a Christian who had his stronghold at Abernethy on the River Tay. He may have been kin to Aidan's Pictish wife.

In the dozen years after the battle of Ardderyd the whole of the North had known peace and the revived Church had put down such firm roots that they proved to be permanent. But in the South disaster had struck the Britons when in 577 the West Saxons under Ceawlin shattered their army at Dyrham on the heights above Bath. The cities of Cirencester and Gloucester fell and the Saxons reached the River Severn and the Bristol Channel. From that time on Dumnonia (Somerset, Devon, Cornwall) was severed from Wales.

In the North the invaders were held in check. As Professor Skene wrote, from the time of Rhydderch Hael "there appears to have been a combination of the Britons of Strathclyde and the Scots of Dalriada against the Saxons and the Picts, the Christian party against the pagan, their common Christianity forming a strong bond of union . . . the Dalriadic king seems to have taken a lead in command of the combined forces." Rhydderch and Urien, the Christian champions, were in their sixties and the fighting troops of the North now looked to Aidan of Dalriada as their combat commander.

As old age weakened Brude's firm rule of Pictland, the old conspirators of Orkney Saxons and Maeatae Picts of the eastern seaboard began their raids again. In 580 King Aidan led a naval expedition against the pirates of the Orkneys and he must have had the backing of Brude and Rhydderch or he could not have dared take the Scots fleet so far from home waters. In 582 he chased the Ulidian Irish out of the Isle of Man and in 583 threw back a Saxon raid into Manaan, Stirlingshire.

During these years Columcille visited King Aidan at his capital of Dunadd, Aidan's Fort, and while there sadly predicted that the King's older sons would fall in battle. "Have you another son?" he asked. Aidan sent for his little boy Eochaid Buidhe, "Yellow Head", and the child ran into Columcille's arms who kissed him saying, "This is the survivor. He shall reign." And from Eochaid descends the Royal Family of Great Britain.

The war with the Saxon-Pict freebooters culminated in the furious battle with the Maeatae Picts, dated by A.O. Anderson about 584 AD. Archaeologists have suggested the battle was near the Bridge of Allan where there is an ancient fort on Dumyat hill, perhaps meaning dun of the Maeatae.†

"Strike the bell!" Columcille called to his servant Diarmit at Iona and its peal brought the Brothers hurrying to the church. "Pray earnestly for King Aidan for now they are going into battle", the Abbot told them. Finally when in his spirit he felt the tide turning, he announced, "Now the barbarians are fleeing and there is victory, but

not a happy one.'' Significantly he called the enemy ''barbarians'', a term used for non-Celtic pagans and would be
applied to Saxons but not to Picts.

The battle was decisive; and it was unhappy. Dalriada's
fighting strength was about two thousand men and in this
battle three hundred and three Scots fell, among them
Arthur and Eochaid Find, the King's sons. Aidan had
dreamed of emulating the great Arthur but with the death
of his own son Arthur, something of the dream died.

The Church's work had gone forward during the years
of peace while Brude, Rhydderch and Aidan had kept the
frontiers, sword in hand. Columcille was grateful to them
for their watch and ward. Yet he had no faith in the sword
as a creative tool; no new world would ever be won by a
sword blade, for those who gain power by force doom
themselves to maintain it by fear. So he viewed violence as
wasted effort, aware that in a crisis the only effective thing
to do was to change the hearts of men. Now the time had
come again for him to take bold and risky action.

Once more the Abbot of Iona led forth his Island Soldiers to do battle in the debatable lands of eastern Alban. His
first move was to make contact with his great ally, Bishop
Mungo of Glasgow. Although they had known of each
other for years, combining in the battle of the faith, they
had never met.

''The Abbot of Hii (Iona)'' narrated Jocelyn, ''desired
earnestly, not once and away, but continually to rejoice in
the light of St. Mungo, to visit him, come into intimacy
and consult regarding things close to his own heart.'' The
Brothers from Iona arrived singing, ''The Saints shall go
from strength to strength, Alleluia!'' Mungo's *eglais cu*

marched out to meet them as far as St. Mungo's Well off Gallowgate, Glasgow, singing "The way of the just is made straight."

Bishop Mungo never ate anything but bread, cheese and milk and no doubt this was the meal he shared with Columcille. Briton and Gael were both in their vigorous sixties and they greatly enjoyed each other's company, marking the occasion by exchanging *bachall*, pastoral staffs. Columcille's staff was treasured for centuries in Ripon Cathedral.

Bishop and Abbot appear to have established a missionary base at Dunkeld and from there launched a six-month combined campaign to win the southern Picts. This is the tradition of Dunkeld Abbey which claims a Columban origin, probably correctly because the Abbot of Dunkeld was always Chief of the Kindred of Columba in Scotland.

The *Amhra* poem tells that Columcille "taught the tribes around the Tay, a river in Alban, and subdued to benedictions the mouths of the fierce ones who dwelt with Tay's High King". Of course, that was Gartnaidh.

Afterwards Columcille established his base on Inchcolm, an Island in the Firth of Forth and the island remained a dependency of Dunkeld for many centuries.

To help in the work of Christianising the eastern Picts, Kenneth of Achabo came across from Ireland. He had marched with Columcille and Comgall into King Brude's fortress at Inverness twenty years before and here he was again, like a good Irishman, spoiling for another fight. He founded a monastery among the east-coast Picts beside the North Sea at Kilrymont, which in time became St. Andrews, the premier bishopric of Scotland.

So the work went forward with Moluag and Drostan in the north, Cathan and Machut, Brendan's disciple, working with the Iona men, and Mungo with his Cumbrians and Welsh from Llanelwy preaching throughout the south. The Picts of the east coast were at last being drawn into the new unity which was coming to all the peoples of Alban and the Cross was planted along the shores of the North Sea, so long the highway of the heathen freebooters.

A cell of Celtic monks on the island of Inchcolm in the Firth of Forth.

For a century or more the Church in Britain had been virtually cut off from Rome. Pilgrimage had been well-nigh impossible due to migrating heathen hordes of Goths, Franks, Huns and Lombards who successively rampaged through the West. The Church itself had been split by schism between Arians and Catholics. But as the sixth century drew to its end communications with Rome, though perilous, were again possible.

About 590 AD Bishop Mungo of Glasgow set off for Rome. What induced a seventy-year-old bishop to undertake the hardships and dangers of a fifteen-hundred-mile journey? There seems only one possible explanation. Ireland, Strathclyde, Alban and the rest of Celtic Britain had been won and reclaimed for the Faith. The next task, formidable but inescapable, was to win the Anglo-Saxons.

Mungo and Columcille must have discussed it together, pondered and prayed about how to do it. The barriers of racial hatred between Celt and Saxon were so high that a direct approach bristled with difficulties. Could Rome gain entry to them on the southern flank? Was it to propose this strategy that Bishop Mungo took the long, long pilgrim's road to Rome?

The Pope that he went to see was Gregory, elected in 590, possibly the greatest of all who have sat in the Fisherman's Chair since Peter. Son of a wealthy senator, he himself was Prefect of Rome in 573 but realised that the huge problems facing his age required a solution far more radical than political action alone. He resigned his post, gave his fortune to the poor, became a monk and turned his home on the Caelian Hill into a monastery.

But his gifts as a statesman were too valuable for the Church to leave him in seclusion and he was appointed papal representative to the Imperial Court in Constantinople. When he returned to Rome about 585 he brought with him a precious relic — the arm of St. Andrew the Apostle. He enshrined it in his home monastery which was thereafter called St. Andrews.

The Pope's interest in the Anglo-Saxons had already been aroused by seeing young Angles for sale in Rome's slave market. "Not Angles, but angels," was his famous remark. "Who is your king?" he asked and they replied, "Aelle of Diera" (560-590). "His song must become Alleluia!" punned Gregory.

A visitor to Rome can still see the marble table in the monastery of St. Andrew at which Gregory entertained his guests and trained his followers. What conversations may have taken place at that table between Pope Gregory and Bishop Mungo? Was it there that the plan was conceived which in 596 sent Augustine, Prior of St. Andrews, with forty monks on the historic mission to Canterbury?

Bishop Mungo returned safely to Glasgow bringing with him Gregory's gift of a bell which is now depicted in the Arms of the City of Glasgow.† Travelling with Mungo's party in all probability were seven messengers sent by the Pope to carry his gifts of a cross and some hymns to Columcille at Iona.

The Abbey of Iona was famous for its unfailing hospitality but it so happened that on the day the papal messengers arrived the Abbey was completely out of food. How mortifying to the courteous Gaelic soul of the Abbot. Adomnan baldly stated, "He prayed and food was miraculously provided." "A somewhat outrageous legend!" expostulated Dr. Lucy Menzies.

But is it? Adomnan reported a miracle, not magic. He omitted the details as being of little concern to men of faith who were his readers, those very details of how, when and what that are of special interest to the modern historian. Did the farmer Colman of Ardnamurchan, finding his herd had increased to more than 105 cows, bring the extra cattle to his friends at Iona, his curragh arriving at the inspired moment? Did Findchan from Dalcros sail over with the surplus of his barley crop?

Today and down the ages, many Christians have experienced God's provision when they trusted that "where He guides, He provides." It is the normal miraculous working of the economics of unselfishness, the economics by which Jesus Himself lived. The Irish saints simply followed His example.

Out of gratitude for his visitors from Rome Columcille wrote his greatest Latin poem, "Altus Prosator". It was an innovation which no one had yet attempted. To make it easier for people to memorise, he used rhyme for the line endings and began each verse with the letter next in sequence in the alphabet. Dr. Douglas Simpson fittingly described the poem as, "the mighty, passionate, insurgent spirit of the man pouring itself forth." A verse of Canon Mitchell's translation caught its cadence.

"Like one who through a sparing sieve
    The precious grain doth slowly pour,
God sendeth down upon the earth
    The cloud-bound waters evermore:
And from the fruitful breasts of heaven,

While changing seasons wax and wane,
The welcome streams that never fail
Pour forth in rich supplies of rain."

The papal messengers returned to Rome taking the "Altus Prosator" back to Pope Gregory, who praised it warmly but commented that it did not sufficiently stress the saving power of the Redeemer. Columcille accepted this valid criticism and wrote a further poem, "In Te Christe". Nevertheless it seems that the "Altus" remained his favourite and he sang it daily as he ground his ration of corn, beginning the first verse as he poured the grain into the quern and ending the last verse with the final twirl of the handle.

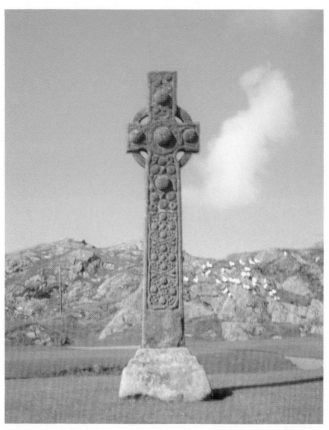

St. Martin's Cross in front of Tor Abb with the flock of white doves.

*Magdalene wiping Christ's feet — detail of Ruthwell Cross
c. 680 AD. Northumbrian work.*

Actions are the fruit of a man's life; his motive is the root. What was Columcille's root motive?

Born a prince of the Gaels, all his life he discharged the duty of his rank. He accepted leadership and made decisions; provided for his followers and his hospitality was open-handed; and he never flinched from the forefront of danger. He fulfilled the best of his royal heritage. But dynastic duty was not his motive.

His religious foundations spread across five hundred miles, housing 4000 or 5000 folk, and on him rested the responsibility for their provision, safety, training and salvation. But organization was not his motive.

He loved his people the Gaels and his labours saved and consolidated the Scots kingdom of Dalriada. But nationalism was not his motive. Indeed he cared as much and fought as hard for other peoples as he did for his own.

As a missionary statesman he stands supreme in the history of the British Isles. His impact on the political and social structure was catalytic and permanent. But politics was not his motive. His influence was enormous and he was greatly loved but neither power or popularity meant anything to him. As for property, he left a cowl, a pectoral cross, some books and a walking stick.

All his life Columcille lived as one of a fellowship of like-minded men and it explains much of his effectiveness. His friendship with Comgall, Brendan, Ciaran, Cormac, Baithen and Kenneth ran too deep for envy or competition. Their comradeship was vital to him because, inspired by the same vision of a world renewed, they could dare the impossible together. Yet their fellowship was not his motive. What then? A personal, intimate devotion to Jesus was the root of everything. He had sought — and been found! "If Christianity isn't a love affair, it's a dull affair" Wilson Carlile used to say.† There was nothing dull about Columcille. His whole passionate nature was absorbed in a love affair with his Saviour and the romance never faded. Busy, travel-weary or persecuted, his spirit was renewed by the Voice which spoke in the silence "to the inner ear of his heart." In a poem he gave away his secret.

> "Sometimes in a lonely cell
> In the presence of God
> The best advice to me has been vouchsafed.
> The King, whose servant I am,
> Will not let anything deceive me."

That God speaks to men who listen is a historical fact attested down the ages by witnesses of the stature of Moses and Daniel, Paul and Francis, Jeanne d'Arc, Wesley, Wilberforce, Lincoln, Nightingale, Booth, Gandhi, Buchman and John XXIII. They received accurate, specific guidance from their Creator. When asked about this experience, Wilson Carlile replied, "Guidance is love in action." The greater the love, the more sensitive the man is to God's guidance.

Columcille loved his *muintir*, monastic family, and it sharpened his perception. One day at Iona he burst out, "It vexes me greatly. Laisran macFeradach is harrassing my monks to put up a large building although they are exhausted." Laisran was the Prior of Durrow in Ireland 200 miles away, but Columcille had sensed in his spirit that an ambitious project was being put ahead of the care for people. Just at that very time some impulse triggered Laisran's conscience and he called off the work and sent the monks to their cells to rest. The Prior learnt his lesson well and was very beloved later when he became the third Abbot of Iona.

As a youth Columcille had asked for Purity and Adomnan wrote, "He preserved his integrity of body and purity of mind all his days." It accounted for his prodigious creativity since no energy drained off into self-indulgence and he did not become self-absorbed. All his satisfaction was found in the joy of Christ's friendship and he needed no compensations for his appetites. The pure in heart see God, they see His purpose working out. The impure do not see Him — which is their tragedy.

"Go quickly and bring Cailtren", the Abbot told his messenger. This man was Prior of the community at Loch Awe on the mainland and when he arrived at Iona the Abbot was at the beach to meet him. "I want you to rest a while" he said, "As one who loves a friend, I have invited you to spend this last time with me." Through unhurried days in the tranquil splendour of the Hebrides the two old comrades walked and talked and at the end of the week Prior Cailtren died.

Free from the earth-bound limitations of materialist plans, Columcille worked both for time and for eternity. Feeding the hungry and freeing the slaves were not ends in themselves but part of the greater plan of preparing men's souls to live in Eternity.

Prophecy was the third gift for which the young prince had prayed. Without question Columcille possessed that very Gaelic talent of "the second sight". It had been with the race for many ages and it is with them still.

Lugbe mocu Blai, a young man of great ability who seems to have served as the Abbot's personal secretary, once asked him about this gift. After swearing him to secrecy, Columcille replied, "There are a few on whom God has bestowed the gift of seeing distinctly, with the scope of the mind miraculously enlarged, the whole circle of the world." Lugbe questioned the need for secrecy and got the very practical answer, "First to avoid boasting; and then to avoid intolerable crowds."

Some time later Lugbe was visiting King Rhydderch of Strathclyde who took him aside and requested him privately to ask Columcille whether the King's enemies would manage to murder him. Lugbe tried to deter him by saying, "Why ask what no man can know?" However, Rhydderch was persistent and in due course Columcille sent him this answer. "Have no fear, for your enermies will in no way harm you. You will die in your own bed with your head on a feather pillow."

And that is how the gallant old Briton died in 603. He had come closer to fulfilling Arthur's dream than any other man; he had kept the faith. Now he lies buried at the foot of the Cloridderck Stone beside Loch Winnoch, west of Glasgow.

Three monks travelling — Papil stone, Shetlands.

Like a line of anchored ships, the Gavellach islands seem moored right in the middle of the Firth of Lorn, half a dozen miles from Mull and from the mainland of Argyll. At the head of the line is Eileach an Naoimh, Rock of the Saint. In storm or fog few boatmen risk landing there and even in fair weather it takes skill to beach a dinghy in the tiny Port Cholumcille. Almost certainly this is the island retreat of Hinba where the Brethren of Iona withdrew for contemplation. The drystone walls of the little Celtic chapel, 21 feet by 11, still stand among the ruined beehive cells of the monks.

This was Columcille's desert place, his holy of holies. Adomnan related, "At one time in Hinba the Holy Spirit poured out upon him in an imcomparable manner for three days and nights while he remained in his house, allowing no one to come in, neither eating nor drinking. Afterwards he confided to a few men that many of the dark and difficult passages of scripture became plain to him. And he lamented that his foster-son Baithen was not there to write down the many mysteries. But Baithen was detained by contrary winds on Eigg."

To join him at Hinba came his greatest friends, Comgall of Bangor, Brendan the Sailor of Clonfert, Cormac O'Lethan and Kenneth of Achabo. It must have been before 578, the year that Brendan died, and it may have been the last time the old sea dog met with him.

Five men of awe-inspiring dedication. As young men they had committed their lives to building colonies of Heaven upon earth. Was it an impossible dream? Other men, without God, have at times built some reasonable facsimiles of Hell on earth! These Irishmen, with God and with heroic tenacity, had persevered until tens of thousands of men and women inhabited colonies which actually were patterns of a God-led new world.

"With one accord they chose Columcille to consecrate the Eucharist", related Adomnan. "Accordingly on the Lord's Day he entered the church along with them. While the Mass was being celebrated, St. Brendan saw (as he afterwards told Comgall and Kenneth), a kind of fiery ball, radiant and very bright that glowed from the head of St. Columba as he stood before the altar."

Maybe the inner light of men such as these sometimes becomes visible. The phenomenon of spiritual light is often spoken of down the ages, the Pentecostal flame and the light on the Damascus road being the best known events. The Light of the world, the mystery at the heart of Christianity, passes understanding.

One day in the evening of his life at Iona, Columcille called his *muintir* around him. "Today I wish to go alone to the western plain of the island. Let no one follow me", he said. He set off across the island until he came to a small clover-clad hill, since known as Cnoc Angel, and at the summit he knelt to pray, hands outstretched to the sky. "But a certain brother, a cunning spy," said Adomnan, "going by another way, took up a hidden position overlooking the plain. Suddenly he saw a marvellous thing. Angels, citizens of the heavenly country, flying with amazing speed down to stand around Columcille as he prayed. And after some converse, as though perceiving themselves watched, quickly sped away."

Back at the monastery "the brother, unable to conceal

his inexcusable sin, fell on his knees for forgiveness. The Abbot took him aside and pledged him never to disclose what he had seen till after he himself was dead."

Citizens of the heavenly country visiting a colony of heaven? A bridge between earth and heaven? Wasn't that what Columcille had given his life to build?

Before any sceptic shrugs it off as mediaeval moonshine, just recall that the belief and record of this man Columcille were strictly biblical. In the New Testament angels appeared to Zacharias, the Virgin Mary and Joseph, the shepherds, Peter, John and Philip, Mary Magdalene, Cornelius the Centurion and Paul — a formidable panel of witnesses. The stories of Columcille confirm that what was true in the first century was also true in the sixth.

And what of the young men of his own day who knew him and who followed him in such numbers? How did they think of him? Fintan, a monk of Iona declared:

"Columcille is not to be compared with philosophers and learned men but with prophets and apostles. The Holy Ghost reigns in him. He has been chosen by God for the good of all. "A sage among sages, a king among kings, a monk among monks, he knows how to be poor of heart among the poor, he can rejoice with the joyful and weep with the grieving. The true humility of Christ is royally rooted in his soul."

An Angel —
Book of Kells, c. 800 A.D.

Fully and movingly Adomnan narrated the story of Columcille's last days. In the early summer of 597 AD he was in his 77th year and felt he was nearing the end of the journey. Too feeble now to walk out to the fields, he rode in a cart drawn by an old white pony to watch his men working on the machair beside the ocean, building stone enclosures to prevent erosion of the soil. When they clustered round the cart he told them, "Last Easter I had a great longing to go to Christ but, lest the Festival of Joy should be turned to sorrow, I chose to put it off a little while".

The next Saturday he set out with his devoted friend and servant Diarmit, companion of all his labours, for a last inspection of the monastery. In the barn he examined the heaps of winnowed corn and congratulated the monks that they had enough to last until the next harvest, then gave his farewell blessing to the barn. But Diarmit became distressed by his master's repeated references to death. "Today is called the Sabbath" the Abbot told him, "the day of rest and today is indeed a Sabbath for me because it is my last day and now I shall rest from my labour. Jesus has invited me and at midnight I shall go to our fathers."

Leaning on Diarmit's arm, he started back towards his own cell but half way he was forced to rest on a grassy bank. Up came the old white pony whinnying and nuzzling its nose against him, although Diarmit tried to shoo him away. "No, no, let him alone, he's fond of me", the Abbot said, "Somehow God has let him know that his master is about to leave." In after years a Cross was raised at this spot and in this century, during excavations, bones were unearthed, thought to be those of a horse.

The old man reached his cell on Tor Abb and stood looking out across the straits to Mull and its massive peak of Ben More.

Raising his arms he blessed Iona with a prophecy:

"Unto this place, small and mean though it be,
Great homage shall yet be paid,
Not only by the Kings and peoples of the Scots,
But by rulers of foreign and barbarous nations
And their subjects.
In great veneration too shall it be held
By holy men of other churches."

Then with the disciplined habit of a lifetime, he sat down at his writing desk and continued copying the Psalter. He was transcribing the 34th Psalm and reached the bottom of the page when he had written the tenth verse: "They that seek the Lord shall not want for any good thing." He laid down his quill saying, "Here I must stop. Baithen must write the rest." (Baithen succeeded him as Abbot and later wrote the next line: "Come, my sons, hear me and I will teach you to reverence the Lord.")

As the sun went down Columcille sat in his cell upon the stone he used for a pillow — now preserved in Iona Abbey — and gave to Baithen a final message for the community. "My children, these are my last words to you. Have genuine love between yourselves, and peace. God, Who comforts the good, will strengthen you and I will pray for you. And he will give you not only your needs for the present life but the eternal good gifts as well."

The midnight bell rang ushering in the Lord's Day and the old man rose and hurried to the church so fast that even the faithful Diarmit lost him in the dark. "Where are you, father?" he called, groping his way forward until he found Columcille stretched out before the altar. He lifted up his head and pillowed it on his lap and the monks as they hastened up with lanterns saw that he was dying. Opening his eyes, he looked from one face to another, joy shining in his smile. Diarmit lifted his right hand and for the last time he made the Saving Sign, the sign of victory.

So passed a prince who had traded a sceptre for a pilgrim's staff. It was Sunday, June 9th, 597 AD. That summer St. Augustine and 40 monks, sent by Gregory the Great from Rome, landed in Kent to begin the conversion of the English.

The rock which was Columcille's*
pillow at Iona, as recorded by
Adomnan.

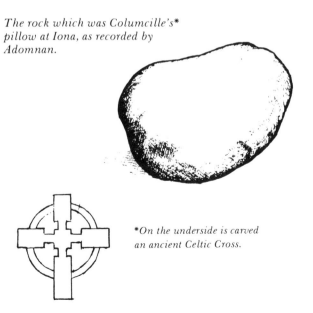

*On the underside is carved
an ancient Celtic Cross.

Lines from the poem of keening
For Columcille, high saint of the Gael,
by Blind Dallan Forgaill, Chief Poet of Ireland.

"It is not a little story this is not a story
        of a fool ·
It is not one district that is keening · nor grief of
        one harpstring ·
he, our rightful head, God's messenger · is dead ·
the teller of words who took away our fear,
        does not return ·
the learned one who taught us silence is gone from us ·
Good his death; he went to God: angels met him ·
he knew the way he was going
he gave kindness for hatred · he broke the battle
        against hunger ·
healer of hearts, satisfier of guests,
Shelter of the naked · comfort of the poor,
their soul's light · a perfect sage who believed Christ ·
Nor went any from this world who more stead-
        fastly bore the Cross ·
It is high his death was"

Wind howled for three days through the thatch of Iona's abbey church, waves crashed foaming up the beach and the Island Soldiers were alone with their dead chief. One of the Brothers had said to him, "After you die the entire population will row over for your funeral and fill Iona". "No, my child" he had answered, "They will not be able to come. Only my *muintir* will celebrate the funeral rites." Weather-wise to the end, he knew a stiff westerly blow often came early in June. And he was right again.

As the sixth century ended a wind seemed to blow away Columcille's generation. *Ard Ri* Aed macAinmire died in 598; Kenneth of Achabo and Baithen of Iona in 600; Comgall of Bangor, Mungo of Glasgow and Rhydderch Hael of Strathclyde in 603.

Some men were catalysts of history. Because they lived, conflicting elements fused and took on new forms; what had been impossible became possible; a new future opened for mankind. Such was the man who is known as Saint Columba of Iona.

In the words of John M. Ross, "He laid the first foundations of Scottish nationality." "Scotland's history may emphatically be said to begin when St. Columba landed at Iona" declared Hume Brown.

It happened because this Irish prince captured the minds and imaginations of warring Scot, Pict and Briton alike by demonstrating a superior idea of what life should be. No longer need loot and revenge be life's goal, for out of Iona came a new breed of men, striding through the glens, eager to give and to serve. A new ideal began to grip the clans and with it came a new unity.

"Under the influence of these teachers", Alice S. Green wrote, "the spirit of racial bitterness was checked, a new intercourse grew up and the peace of Columcille rested on the people." And Professor Skene's studies showed, "During 150 years since the Picts were converted there is hardly a battle between Picts and Scots. Had they viewed each other as hostile races it is difficult to account for the more powerful Picts permitting a small colony of Scots to remain undisturbed. Prior to Colomba's mission they were endeavouring to expel them but after that date there existed a powerful element of peace. As long as that influence lasted the Picts remained at peace with the Scots."

Gaelic was a written language, thanks to the monks, and it was the vehicle of teaching in the monastic schools throughout Alban. Thus it became the accepted tongue of educated men and the Pictish dialects faded away. North of the Firths of Forth and Clyde and Picts and Scots, united by a common faith, a common speech and increasingly by intermarriage, began to merge into one people. The process was gradual but irreversible. The Scottish nation was coming into being.

St. Columba was buried in the tiny chapel at the west end of Iona Abbey. There is a stone coffin there today thought to be the one in which his body first lay. The Kings of the Scots and the Picts were brought to Iona for burial close to their own special saint and a never-ending stream of pilgrims made their way by foot and boat to this shrine out of devotion to the man who had become the very soul of the people.

Thus far we have been led by Adomnan's superb record. Now it ends. But the story is immediately taken up by Adomnan's friend, "the father of English history", Bede, monk of the Benedictine monastery of Jarrow, Northumbria. He tells us what had been happening in Rome during the last years of St. Columba and St. Mungo. There momentous events were afoot as the strategy of Pope Gregory the Great took shape.

Sometimes it is easy to imagine that the Papacy has always been powerful and wealthy, wielding undisputed authority, but in the time of Pope Gregory the facts were otherwise. The seat of the Roman Empire had long since shifted to Constantinople and even the Western Empire was ruled from Ravenna. Goths and Vandals had sacked Rome and it had been taken and re-taken. Its aqueducts were ruined and the water, pouring from the broken channels, had turned the valley bottoms into malarial swamps. From a million the population had shrunk to 50,000 and they huddled close to the river as the muddy Tiber was their only water supply. The glory had departed. Only the Papacy remained. But its authority was denied by half Europe, including northern Italy, which followed the Arian heresy.

This was the state of affairs which faced Gregory when in 590 he was elected Pope. He had personal difficulties too. He was often in agony from gastric pain and exhausted by a chronic fever. A sick man in a ruined city. Yet his indomitable love reached out to win the heathen English, whom St. Gildas had called "a race hateful to God and man."

Gregory longed to lead the mission to England himself but when he was elected Pope it was impossible. To go in his stead he chose the Prior of his monastery of St. Andrews. His name was Augustine. With him went forty picked volunteers.

They set out from Rome in 596 with high resolve but by the time they reached Gaul, Bede said, "they became appalled at the idea of going to a barbarous, fierce, pagan nation of whose very language they were ignorant. They unanimously agreed that the safest course was to send Augustine back to request Gregory to recall them." These were brave men as their later lives proved. If they quailed, the perils must have been enough to daunt the boldest. But what if Gregory had recalled them?

Instead he wrote a letter of compassionate, firm encouragement. "Gregory, servant of the servants of God. My very dear sons, it is better never to undertake a high enterprise than to abandon it when once begun. With God's help, carry on. Do not be deterred by the journey or by what men say. The greater the labour, the greater will be the glory. Although my office prevents me working at your side, I long to do so and I hope to share in your reward. God keep you safe, my dearest sons."

Augustine and his men sailed for England.

English Dawn

The Venerable Bede of Jarrow sharpening his quill — from a codex at Engelberg Abbey, Switzerland.

At the eastern nub of Kent was the Isle of Thanet where Hengist and his three boatloads of Saxon mercenaries had landed, at the beginning of the conquest of England. It was fitting that Augustine and his clergy landed at the same spot in 597. They had come to see the great-great-grandson of Hengist, King Ethelbert of Kent, the most powerful ruler whose sway extended as far north as the Humber. He had married Bertha, daughter of King Charlbert of the Franks. She was a Christian and insisted on practising her religion with the aid of her chaplain, Bishop Liudhard. She was the first of a number of royal brides whose courageous, lonely witness at a pagan court opened the way for the conversion of England.

The royal party crossed over to Thanet to receive the Pope's mission, the King warily sitting in the open lest magic spells be put upon him inside a house. Behind a silver cross and a picture of Christ painted on a board, the monks approached, singing. After listening courteously to Augustine, the King said, "Your words and promises are fair but they are new. I cannot abandon the age-old beliefs that all the English hold. But you have travelled far, you are sincere and we will not harm you. Your needs will be supplied and you may speak to the people."

In a house at Canterbury which the King gave them, the little group of foreigners set about living the life of the primitive church, praying, teaching and accepting only their bare necessities. There was a ruined church built in Roman times and dedicated to St. Martin and here they daily met for Mass with the Queen and her chaplain. And all the while English eyes watched every move they made.

First a few, then a number came for instruction because they admired the simplicity of their lives. Finally Ethelbert himself believed and was baptised, but declared that no one must feel compelled to follow his example as Christ's service can only be accepted freely.

Nevertheless the work of conversion now went forward rapidly and Augustine went back to Arles in Gaul to be consecrated as the first Archbishop of Canterbury. Pope Gregory joyfully sent him the pallium, granting him full authority. "We commit to your charge all the bishops of Britain. Instruct the unlearned, strengthen the weak, correct the misguided." He added the sage advice that idols should be destroyed but that the temples themselves, if well built, should be dedicated to the true God. The people would more readily flock to their accustomed places of worship.

Gregory in 601 sent an important reinforcement to the English mission: Mellitus the Abbot of St. Andrews, Justus, Rufinianus and Paulinus, all personally picked and trained by himself.

In 603, one year before he died, Augustine made a personal appeal to the Britons to help in the work of winning the English for Christ. He travelled to the western frontier of Wessex where under Augustine's Tree (at Aust on the River Severn) he met the Bishops of the Britons and asked for their help. But they refused to have anything to do with him, accusing the Archbishop of pride because he did not rise from his seat to greet them. Perhaps the Roman was tactless, yet the huffy self-importance of the Bishops sounds exactly like the behaviour which St. Gildas had condemned so scathingly fifty years before. So the great opportunity passed the Britons by for ever.

But before Augustine departed he put the issue squarely before them. "If you do not preach the Gospel to the English, you will suffer death at their hands" — a prediction which came grimly true a dozen years later.

By then, the great Pope Gregory had laid down his task, for he died in 604. Towards the end of his days he wrote happily, "The tongue of Britain has begun to cry Alleluia!" And later the Englishman Bede wrote of him, "We may rightly call Gregory our own apostle." Upon his tomb in St. Peters, Rome, were carved the words:

"To Christ he led the English, by God's grace
Swelling Faith's armies with a new-won race."

Looking back it is easy to see that the Britons' best defence was to Chritianise the English and thus win their respect and gratitude. Illtud, David and Cadoc would have seized the opportunity. But recalling what was happening in Britain just then, it is not surprising that the Britons did not see it that way.

Northumbria was pushing out in all directions under the aggressive leadership of King Ethelfrid. About 600 AD the Britons mobilized their full strength for a counter-attack against him. They rallied their army in Gododdin, the Lothians of Scotland. Young nobles came as volunteers from as far as Cornwall. The battle array was spear-headed by three hundred mounted men, Britannia's finest warriors. Arthur's calvalry seem to have been fast and formidable because they were well mounted but since his day horse-breeding had been neglected and the Britons' horses were of poor quality.

Aneiran, a poet of Cumbria, rode with the army and told its story in his epic poem "Gododdin" which gave an air of gay knight errantry to the venture. The troops swept south, probably following the old Roman road from Camelon, near Falkirk, through Newstead and Corbridge until they reached Catterick. Here Ethelfrid and his Northumbrians barred the way.

"The men went to Catterick with the dawn,
   Swift their army, pale mead was their feast
      And it was their poison . . .
Three hundred men battling according to plan,
   Their high courage shortened their lives . . .

The men went to Catterick in column, a force of steeds,
  Blue armour and shields, javelins aloft,
Keen lances, bright coats of mail and swords,
  Together they attacked ..."

The English who usually fought in the open, had taken position within the old Roman fortifications. The Britons made the mistake of launching cavalry against entrenched infantry — something Arthur would never have done.

Their gallant cavalry charges broke against the English shield-wall and few of the light-hearted warriors lived to return home. The Votadini tribe of the Lothians had sent their whole manpower and they were all wiped out. The tribe virtually ceased to exist.

The disaster at Catterick exposed the kingdom of Strathclyde to an imminent threat of invasion. The Britons of the Green Standard rallied all the allies they could find. The Scots came from Dalriada, and an Irish contingent from Ulster. The command of the mixed force was given to King Aidan and he was granted the princely title of "Guletic". On the height of land in the Cheviot Hills at Dawstane, near Hawick, Aidan faced Ethelfrid in 603. On the right wing the Irish at first advanced but on the left the Scots were driven in. Aidan's son Domangart was killed and the retreat became general. "From this time forth none of the Kings of Scots ventured to come in battle against the nation of the English" wrote Bede.

Aidan never recovered from the blow and died soon after, either in 606 or 609. There are indications that he handed the kingdom over to his son and withdrew into religion. How dark the future must have seemed to him. Policies of a lifetime lay in ruins; Arthur's dream, to

Vikings in 806 AD massacred sixty-eight monks at Martyrs' Bay, Iona. The Abbot and Brethren, carrying the saint's body, with-drew to Kells, Ireland.

Lindisfarne "a second Iona among the English".

which he had dedicated his life, was dead, dead as his sons who had fallen in the struggle. Had it all been in vain? He could not know that out of this military disaster would come a momentous opportunity and the greatest of all Iona's victories.

Aidan did not live to see the final defeat which fell upon the Britons in 616. The Northumbrians were threatening to cut right across Britain to the Irish Sea and the Britons drew up their army in front of Chester to halt them. 2,000 monks from Bangor-is-Coed in Wales massed on a nearby hill to pray for victory. Ethelfrid asked what they were doing, then said, "If they are praying against us, they are fighting against us." He launched his first attack at the monks, killing 1200 of them, and this massacre unnerved the main army which broke and fled.

Chester fell, Wales was cut off from the Britons of the North, and Britannia was no more.

In Kent 616 was also a black year. Ethelbert died and was buried beside Queen Bertha in St. Martin's Porch at Canterbury. His son Eadbald reigned in his stead. Unlike his father, the new king was no saint. He lived openly with his step-mother and when Archbishop Laurence remonstrated, he told him to pack his bags and be gone. Bishops Justus and Mellitus had already fled to Gaul and it seemed to Laurence, as he prepared to go into exile, that twenty years of work was ending in total failure.

On the last night before leaving, the Archbishop made his bed in the deserted church at Canterbury and prayed himself to sleep. In a dream he saw St. Peter who demanded how he dared abandon his flock to the wolves. "Have you forgotten my example, that I suffered chains and death for His little ones?"

It was a "Quo Vadis?" experience for the Archbishop. In the morning he faced the King with such courage and conviction that he won his man. Eadbald was converted and baptised, broke off his illicit union and recalled the exiled Bishops.

Ethelfrid of Northumbria, victor of Catterick, Dawstane and Chester, was at the peak of his power. But, like all heathen rulers, he lived in dread of rivals and he especially feared his brother-in-law Edwin, son of Aelle of Deira. Even as an exile he pursued him with paid assassins, hounding him from one refuge to another.

But after the battle of Chester Ethelfrid made a mistake; he let his troops go home with their booty. Edwin saw his chance and, scraping together a small striking force, he attacked and killed Ethelfrid at the river Idle before he could mobilise his army again.

One day a refuge, the next England's leading king! Edwin ruled both parts of Northumbria: Deira, his father's realm, lying between the rivers Humber and Tees; and Bernicia, all the North Sea coast from the Tees up to the newly conquered area of Gododdin on the Firth of Forth. To protect the new conquest in the north Edwin founded a fortified town on a massive rock beside the Forth, called by the Britons "Mynedd Agned" — "Hill of the plain" and named it Edwin's Burg — Edinburgh.

Edwin sought a wife among his kinsmen of the royal house of Kent. King Eadbald agreed to the marriage of his sister, Ethelberga, nicknamed Tata, but only on condition that she could be attended by Christians and have a chaplain. She chose Bishop Paulinus as her chaplain, one of Pope Gregory's hand-picked men, tall, dark, stooped, with a hooked nose and awe-inspiring presence. And so Tata went north just as her mother had, a Christian bride going to a heathen court.

On her first Easter Day in the strange land, 626, Tata gave birth to a daughter. In the great hall the king was rejoicing when an assassin lunged at him with a poisoned dagger. His counsellor Lilla sprang forward and took the fatal blow in his own body. Shaken by the death of his friend, grateful for his own escape and the safe delivery of his wife, Edwin promised the Queen that the babe Eanfled should be dedicated to Christ.

"Edwin was by nature a prudent man who often sat alone in silent converse for long periods, turning over in his inmost heart what he should do" Bede wrote. Finally he summoned his council, the Witanagemot, to Goodmanham near York to decide whether to accept the new faith. It was here that an earlderman made the famous comparison of man's life to the flight of a sparrow into a warm, lighted banquet hall, then out into the night again.

But the great surprise was Coifi, the pagan High Priest. "I have long realised that there is nothing in our worship," he admitted. "The more I sought for truth, the less I found. None has been more devout than I and if our gods had power surely they would have favoured me, but others got greater honours. (This reveals the *quid pro quo* basis of pagan religion). But this new teaching reveals truth that gives blessing in this life and eternal happiness. Our altars are of no use and should be burned. I will do it myself!"

Borrowing a stallion and weapons from the King, Coifi galloped away to smash the idols while the crowds stared, quite sure he had gone mad.

On Easter Day 627 Edwin and his nobles came to the little log church of St. Peter at York and were baptised by

Paulinus. All that summer the Bishop worked from dawn
to dusk at Yeavering and Catterick teaching and baptising
thousands. To help him came Bishop Rhun, grandson of
King Urien of Cumbria, who was St. Mungo's successor.
Perhaps as a young monk in Rome Paulinus had met
Mungo. Anyway, here was one Briton who entered
wholeheartedly into the task of preaching the Gospel to
the English. At Catterick, where the flower of Britain's
youth had fallen, Briton and Roman together baptised a
whole people who had been foes. Aelle's son and all his
folk were singing Alleluia!

For six years Northumbria enjoyed peace as it had never
known and it was said that in Edwin's reign "a woman
could carry her new-born child across the island from sea
to sea without fear of harm."

Suddenly it was over. Cadwalla of Gwynedd, a nominal
Christian, made common cause with pagan Penda of
Mercia.† In 633 they killed Edwin at Hatfield and sent fire
and sword from end to end of Northumbria. Bishop Paulinus hurried the widowed Tata and baby Eanfled away by
ship to the safety of Kent.

Far off on Iona meanwhile the strangest part of the story
had been quietly taking shape. In 617 two refugee children
arrived at the island asking for Church sanctuary. The
kindly Brethren took them in and, as they did for
hundreds of waifs, fostered them and gave them a home,
an education and a faith in God. The older boy, Oswald,
was about thirteen, his little brother Oswy only five. They
were English, the orphaned sons of the mighty Ethelfrid
of Northumbria.

The Abbot of Iona at that date was Fergna Brit (603-

623), a close kinsman of St. Columba. He and his successor Segine cared for the boys for fifteen year by which time Oswald had grown to be, in Bede's words, "a man beloved by God." When he was 23 he would have heard with interest that his uncle King Edwin had become a Christian. But it did not directly affect him because his elder brother, who was living among the Picts, had first claim to inherit the throne.

In 633 everything changed. Edwin was slain and Oswald's elder brother, trying to regain the throne, was slain too. Oswald was now the heir and he felt deeply his duty to rescue his tyrannized fellow countrymen and continue the work of conversion. He enlisted a small force of exiles and refugees and, with the Cross as his standard, marched into Northumbria.

Cadwalla's powerful army was encamped just north of the Roman Wall but carelessly posted since Oswald's small brigade seemed to pose no threat. But Oswald, greatly encouraged by a dream of St. Columba, determined to risk a night attack. Surprise was total and in the rout Cadwalla of Gwynedd met his end. The victory was known as the battle of Heavenfield.

What had young Oswald learnt of statecraft during his years at Iona? Apparently a good deal because he became England's most renowned king until the time of Alfred the Great. The whole island acknowledged him as Bretwalda, High King. It was his wisdom that guided the people through the spiritual upheaval of conversion. "Although he reached such a height of power", wrote Bede, "Oswald was always humble, kindly and generous to the poor and strangers."

His first act as King of Northumbria was to ask the Brethren of Iona to send a bishop to teach his people. Bishop Corman, who was sent, proved to be one of those clever men who put the hay too high for the horses to get at it. He retreated to Iona grumbling that the English were ungovernable and obstinate. A Scot named Aidan suggested "Maybe our Brother was too severe. Why not begin with the milk of simple teaching, as the Apostles did, and afterwards feed them with the loftier precepts?" All eyes turned towards Aidan and needless to say he was soon off to Northumbria as bishop.

In every way Aidan was the true heir and successor of St. Columba. Bede portrayed him fully, adding "I admire and love all these things about Aidan." The way he lived melted the obstinate Saxon hearts. "On Aidan's arrival King Oswald gave him the island of Lindisfarne, near Bamburgh, his capital. As the tide ebbs and flows, twice a day it becomes an island. The King listened readily to Aidan and they set about establishing the Church throughout the kingdom. Aidan was not fluent in English and it was delightful to see the King himself interpreting to his thanes, for he spoke Gaelic perfectly."

"Aidan gave his clergy an inspiring example of self-discipline and continence and the highest recommendation of his teaching was that he and his followers lived as they taught. He never sought or cared for worldly possessions and loved to give away to the poor whatever he received from wealthy folk. In town or country, he travelled on foot, stopping to talk with anyone he met, high or low, pagan or Christian. All who walked with him were expected to meditate and read Scripture. If invited to dine with the King, he took along a couple of clergy, ate sparingly and left as soon as possible. If wealthy people did wrong he would not keep quiet out of respect or fear but corrected them outspokenly. If the rich gave him money, he used it to ransom slaves. Many he ransomed later became priests."

King and Bishop: how tales about them must have gone the rounds in hall and hut, more marvellous than the sagas of the scalds. Bede related "The story is told how on the Feast of Easter one year, Oswald sat down to dine with Aidan. A rich meal on a silver dish was set before him when his almoner told him that there was a crowd of needy people sitting in the road outside. Oswald at once ordered his dinner to be taken out to them and the silver dish broken up and distributed. The Bishop, deeply moved, grasped the King's hand, exclaiming "May this hand never wither!"

But Aidan was sometimes an upsetting guest. Visiting King Oswin who at the time ruled Deira, he received the gift of a fine horse with handsome trappings so that he would no longer have to walk. Soon afterwards Aidan met a beggar, dismounted and gave him the horse, harness and all. That night at dinner Oswin protested "Why did you give away the royal horse? Weren't less valuable beasts good enough for beggars?" Aidan was shocked. "Your Majesty, what are you saying? Is that child of a mare more valuable to you than a child of God?"

For a long while Oswin stood staring into the fire. Then impulsively, taking off his sword, knelt before the Bishop, saying "I will never again question how much of our bounty you give away to God's children."

Lindisfarne grew into a second Iona among the English, pulsing with life. The best and boldest of the youth made their way to the island, eager to enlist. Aidan picked out twelve young men and gave them his special attention; among them were the brothers Chad and Cedd who were to be the pioneer bishops of the Mercians and East Saxons, and Eata who founded Melrose abbey.

This was Bede's picture of Lindisfarne. "There were very few buildings except the church; indeed, no more than met the bare requirements of a seemly way of life. They had no property except cattle and immediately gave to the poor any money they received, for they had no need to amass money to provide lodging for important people. Such as visited the church came only to pray and hear the word of God. If they remained for a meal, they were content with the plain daily food of the Brothers. These teachers' only concern was to satisfy the soul, not the belly.

"Accordingly the religious dress was held in high esteem. When a priest visited a village the people quickly gathered for he came solely to preach, baptise, visit the sick and care for souls."

King Oswald married the daughter of Cynigils of Wessex who had been converted by Bishop Birinus, sent by the

Pope to the West Saxons. When he was baptised, Oswald stood as his godfather. It is an interesting example of the interlocking missionary efforts from north and south. Some books imply that there was competition to the point of hostility but the records do not bear this out. Instead they show the Romans and Celts striving toward a common objective like two corps of one army.

Another example can be seen among the East Saxons where the Faith had great difficulty putting down permanent roots. Sibert, the heir-apparent to the throne, found it safer to live in exile in Gaul. Here he was converted and became a devout and learned Christian. When he returned to mount the throne of the East Saxons he brought with him a Burgundian, Bishop Felix from Canterbury to found a boys's school. A renowned Irish monk Fursey arrived to help with the work of conversion and Sibert encouraged him to found monasteries. When at last the King felt the Church was firmly planted, he resigned the throne in favour of his brother and became a monk.

But the neighbouring kingdom of Mercia was ruled by Penda, a cunning implacable enemy of the Christians. When he caught some converts preaching in his territory he buried them under a huge pile of stones at a village still called Stone. In 635 he attacked the East Saxons. Badly outnumbered, the Saxons turned for leadership to their ex-King and at their urging Sibert placed himself in the front rank and faced death in the pagans' charge. But he refused to carry any weapons except a walking stick — a rather English touch.

In 642 Penda tried conclusions with Oswald and killed the Christian champion at the battle of Oswestry. He was only thirty-eight. But Oswald dead was almost as potent a force as when he was alive, becoming a legend and a hero to all the English.

His brother Oswy inherited Bernicia and Edwin's son Oswin ruled Deira. Oswy was less of a credit to Iona than his brother but he changed and grew with adversity. His first wife was Rieinmelth, a great-niece of Bishop Rhun and great-grand-daughter of Urien of Cumbria. Through her, Cumbria passed peacefully into the domain of Northumbria. Their son Alchfrid was educated in Ireland and Iona and later on made an excellent king. Surprisingly he married Cyniburg, daughter of the pagan Penda and became great friends with her brother Peada. Not even Penda's own children were immune to the holy infection spreading from Iona!

Peada, "a noble young man well deserving the title of king" said Bede, was governing the Middle Saxons near London. He travelled to Bamburgh to ask Oswy's permission to marry his daughter. Oswy refused unless he first accepted the Faith. But Peada had been talking deeply with Alchfrid and replied, "I will gladly become a Christian even if the princess refuses me."

He was baptised with all his thanes and returned to Mercia, taking with him the priests Cedd, Adda, Betti and the Scot Diuma from Iona. At Sandbach near Crewe still stand the "preaching crosses" whose carvings show figures of the monks on their mission to Mercia. Even his father Penda no longer forbade preaching the Faith in his land, though he grumbled that he despised those who accepted it but didn't live it.

Oswy, a widower, married a second time. He sent to

Kent to ask Eanfled, Edwin's daughter, to be his wife. So the child born to Edwin and Tata on Easter Day returned to Northumbria as Queen, probably in 642 when she was seventeen.

Friction developed between Bernicia and Deira which came to blows in 651. Oswin was captured by Oswy who promptly had him executed. There was nothing unusual about that; for centuries it had been the normal way to dispose of political rivals. But what was unusual was the huge outcry — "universal disgust" Bede called it — that an Iona-trained king should kill his cousin. It broke the saintly Bishop Aidan's heart for he loved both boys and he died eleven days later. Aidan of Lindisfarne, heir of Columba of Iona, who more than any other made the English a Christian people.

Oswy deeply and bitterly repented this evil act and in atonement built a monastery at Gilling where daily prayers were said for the slain and slayer. But the execution destroyed the towering moral ascendancy which Oswald had bequeathed to his dynasty. Penda once more unleashed his war dogs so savagely that Oswy was compelled, said Bede, "to offer an incalculable quantity of regalia as the price of peace. But the treacherous King Penda refused, declaring he would wipe out the entire Northumbrian nation from highest to lowest. Oswy turned for help to the mercy of God, saying "If the heathen refuse our gifts, let us offer them to the Lord."

Oswy and his son Alchfrid gave battle to a Mercian army thirty times greater than their own beside the flooded Winwaed stream in the area of Leeds and won a resounding victory. Here old Penda died.

Now Lindisfarne poured out its men all across England. Chad went to be bishop to the Mercians at Lichfield, his brother Cedd to the East Saxons at Tilbury. From Malmesbury the Irish monk Maeldubh was converting the West Saxons; there were Irish monks at Glastonbury; and among the South Saxons at Bosham. The Archbishop's chair at Canterbury was occupied by Deusdedit, the first Englishman to hold that office.

One century had passed since St. Columba had stepped ashore in the threatened beach-head of Dalriada. And now the warming rays from Iona, like and English dawn, were lighting the furthest corners of the British Isles.

"The Celts held out against the Teutonic savages until they ceased to be savages. Civilization never entirely perished in Britain, night never extended from sea to sea. The country became England, not a wild, heathen Saxondom." This profoundly true assessment was made by Geoffrey Ashe.

Ninian and Patrick, Illtud and Arthur, Cadoc and Finnian, Rhydderch and Mungo, Columcille and Aidan of Lindisfarne. This was their victory.

*Seventh century "preaching crosses' at Sandbach near Crewe
commemorate the mission to Mercia of Prince Peada and monks
from Iona and Lindisfarne.*

The winning of the English was the direct outcome of St. Columba's lifework, in conjunction with his great allies St. Mungo and St. Gregory. Rather than compare what each did separately, it is more to the point to recognize what they achieved together.

Under the inspiration brought by the Celtic and Roman clergy, the English race suddenly burst into flower displaying gifts of music and poetry, literature and sculpture never before suspected. A Saxon ploughman, Caedmon, startled the learned of his day by revealing great poetic genius. Scholars like Aldhelm of Malmesbury won Europe-wide reputations, and Bede must surely rank with Chaucer and Shakespeare among the very best. In him two streams blended together. The missionary passion of the Gaels from Iona, and the disciplined devotion of the Benedictines from Rome.

A beautiful symbol of this awakening is the Ruthwell Cross which stands near Dumfries, Scotland. It is a twenty-foot-tall "preaching cross", the Gospel carved in stone, and it tells the Bible stories as clearly today as when it was first raised in about 670 AD. The concept is Celtic but the superb workmanship is Northumbrian and shows the influence of Roman art. The narrow sides of the cross are inscribed in runic script with the poem "Dream of the Holy Rood" attributed to the ploughman poet Caedmon of Whitby (d.680):

> "Was I there with blood bedabbled,
> Gushing grievous from His side
> When His ghost He had up-rendered? . . .

Significantly the Ruthwell Cross stands near Hoddam which for years was the centre of St. Mungo's work in Cumbria. This area had come under the rule of the Northumbrian kings but apparently the Celtic clergy had continued their service with unabated vitality, working in harmony with the English newcomers.

A mighty hunger for learning took possession of the young men of England and, in the words of Aldhelm, "they crowded across to Ireland in fleets." The Irish monks received them with great kindness and not only taught them free of charge but supplied them with books, food and lodging. This was in the best tradition of the *Filidh* who held that wisdom was common property to be shared. But the open hospitality of the Irish to this crowd of foreign youths demonstrated "love thy neighbour" applied on a nation-wide scale.

It was a quality of life, not just book learning, which was the magnet. "What most arrests our attention", said John T. McNeill, "is the astonishing flow of youth into the monastic life which drew men with an irresistible attraction". The monks". . . found themselves pursued by throngs of young men eager to follow their example."

What was taking place in Ireland was a spiritual and cultural combustion hardly equalled elsewhere in history. From this little-known island on the rim of the outer ocean suddenly burst forth an illumination bright as the Northern Lights and its rays flooded the continent.

Europe was in collapse at the time this happened. Great wars, wave after wave of pillaging invaders and catastrophic plagues had overturned all political stability and the writ of law. That a civilizing counter-force should come to the rescue from far-away Ireland is one of the most improbable twists of history.

The Romanized peoples still thought of the Irish as the thieving savages described by Gildas. "With villainous faces covered with hair, they pour out of their curraghs like a swarm of worms." A brawling, irascible race of whom L.G. Pine has said "The Gaels were never united." And he was almost right. But for one short, shining age the Gaels generated a spiritual power so uniting, so generous that it saved and remade Europe.

The Golden Age, as books call it, was not an accident. It was created, beginning when St. Patrick brought forgiveness to Ireland, chasing snakes of vengeance out of Irish hearts and freeing their creative genius for constructive tasks. A century later the Clonard men caught the imagination of the youth, educated and disciplined them into an effective force. Then came St. Columba's mission to Iona which charted a new course for the Irish. Their message was now "for export".

So began what Alice S. Green called "The most remarkable missionary effort known to Europe for its enterprise and long endurance. From this time the succession of missionaries and teachers never failed during four hundred years. Their work restored culture and the Christian faith to shattered Europe. They founded schools, taught the art of writing and skilled methods of agriculture. One of the wonders of European history will always be the story of the Irish monks and the charity with which they gave so liberally."†

THE WINNING OF ENGLAND

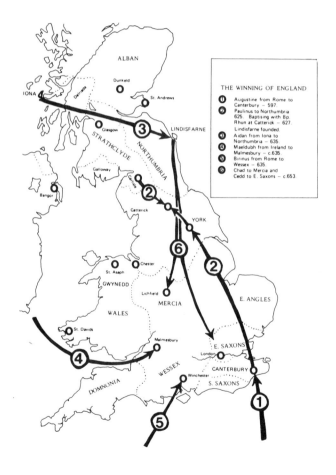

THE WINNING OF ENGLAND

① Augustine from Rome to
Canterbury – 597.

② Paulinus to Northumbria
625. Baptising with Bp.
Rhun at Catterick – 627.
Lindisfarne founded.

③ Aidan from Iona to
Northumbria – 635.

④ Maeldubh from Ireland to
Malmesbury – c.635.

⑤ Birinus from Rome to
Wessex – 635.

⑥ Chad to Mercia and
Cedd to E. Saxons – c.653.

They were called Peregrini — travellers abroad — these Irishmen who went into voluntary exile "for the love of God". Few ever saw the Emerald Isle again. They followed an unknown road ignorant of where it would lead them, certain only that they were being led. Armed with nothing but a few books and a prayer bell, they travelled among barbarous, warring tribes and claimed them as children of God. The invasion of the Peregrini was the total opposite of every other invasion Europe has known. These invaders were contemptuous of loot, power or glory or anything but the salvation of their fellow men. It was the most daring, persistent, beneficial and long-sustained invasion on record.

The prototype of the Peregrini was St. Columbanus (c540-615) a Leinster boy who as a youth was trained by Sennell of Cloninnis, one of the "Twelve Apostles of Ireland". He sent him on to Bangor where for twenty years he worked with Comgall. He certainly must have known Columcille, Brendan, Moluag and the other pioneer Abbots who were his models and inspiration.

In 590 AD Columbanus was 40, a noted scholar, expected to succeed Comgall as Abbot of Bangor. But he felt an inner summons to set out for Gaul. Asked what was his aim, he answered "The salvation of many and a solitary spot for myself."

Columbanus picked a dozen friends to go with him, as St. Columba had when he went to Iona. The best known were St. Gall of Switzerland and St. Deicola of Lure. They took nothing from Bangor but the discipline which was their rule of life. They were backed by no Board of Missions and could draw on no funds but trusted the Almighty to guide and provide for them. They set sail for Brittany, landed and marched inland. The only tongue they could communicate in was Latin. When a Frankish king offered them a grant of good farm land they declined it, saying they had no wish to deprive others of it. Instead they kept on travelling till they came to a ruined Roman fort at Annegray in the wild Vosges mountains and there they settled.

At their fort the Irish worked, prayed — and starved. They were finally reduced to eating the bark of trees. Then one Brother fell gravely ill and urgently needed nourishing food if he was to recover. Together the community laid their plight before God. That day a man rode into the fort leading a horse laden with food. He had come, he said, to ask the Brothers to pray for his wife who was ill with fever. They prayed with him and when he got home he found his wife sitting up to welcome him.

From then on people came to Annegray in growing crowds. Miracles multiplied as they cured the sick or quarrelsome, the drunk or greedy, baptised children and cared for the old and dying. Young men came asking to be trained as monks in such numbers that new monasteries were opened at Luxeuil and Fontaine.

But the renown of Columbanus disconcerted some of the worldly bishops and the purity of his life enraged the debauched young King of Austrasia. Gaul was in a sorry state and, as St. Gregory of Trours chronicled, many bishops were merely state administrators, taking sides in the squabbles of princes and profiting from them. The year that Columbanus arrived at Annegray, the bishopric of Paris was openly bought by a merchant as a business investment.

Such men could not publicly attack the holy life of the Abbot of Annegray so instead they attacked his Celtic custom of observing Easter according to the old-fashioned system of reckoning still used in Ireland.

Persecuted and exiled by the King, Columbanus was quite undaunted and as a contemporary said of him "He hurled the fire of Christ wherever he could without concerning himself with the blaze it caused." Exile was merely an opportunity to hurl fire somewhere else and he left a fiery trail through France, Germany, Austria, Switzerland and north Italy. He did for these countries what St. Aidan had done for England.

In the judgement of Pope Pius XI (d.1939) "The more experts study the obscure problems of the Middle Ages the clearer it becomes that the renaissance of Christian learning in France, Germany and Italy was due to the work and zeal of St. Columbanus."

Columbanus, product and heir of the Clonard men, spearheaded the invasion of the Peregrini. Before the seventh century closed he and his followers had founded ninety-four monasteries across Europe. But this book cannot attempt even an outline of his life.

Franks and Germans joined the floods of English crossing over to Ireland to study at Clonmacnois, Glendalough and the other famous Abbey schools. But the traffic in the other direction was heavier, as Peregrini sailed to Europe in hundreds and then in thousands to carry on the civilizing work Columbanus had started. Dedicated Englishmen joined them, such as St. Willibord who was Irish-

trained, and St. Boniface who together spread the Faith
through Holland and the Rhineland.

Peregrini were not adventurous youngsters with wander-
lust. Most had spent a score of years under strict monastic
rule and their characters and ability had been tested. They
were better read and better Latin scholars than most they
would meet on the mainland. They did not go representing
any institution but as individuals obeying an inner command. Obedience was a prime virtue in their rule of life but
it was valued for its spiritual merit not for organizational
efficiency and although they respected the hierarchy of the
Church, they looked to no one as their leader but Christ.

"Whatever the locals thought of the immigrant Irishmen", wrote Brendan Lehane, "they must have been
impressed. Into an atmosphere of shift and deception
walked bands of Irish with a clear sense of purpose. It had
nothing to do with vendettas or luxury, making money or
winning territory. Worship came first, but good worship
presupposed good health. They revived long-term farming methods, fed themselves and gave provisions to the
needy. They were healthy in mind as much as in body,
gave no precedence to material things, and showed little
fear or favour to rich or poor.

"To a country that was sick for want of principle or
criterion, the sight of a file of these cloaked figures with
their satchels of willow osiers was a welcome one. Their
reputations went before them and they were talked about
by villagers, chiefs and kings."

But they took no part in politics. "As guests in the
world, do not get entangled in earthly desires" warned
Columbanus. However, they spoke out boldly enough to

correct political leaders if they were not upright, since just laws for the people could not be expected from a ruler who was not moral and just himself.

The Peregrini were at home wherever they found themselves. "Home is not a place" taught Columbanus "but a road to be travelled." So, however far-ranging the journey, they were always on their way home. They certainly were far-ranging. Their tinkling prayer bells were heard in Carthage and Iceland and the Norsemen later found their traces in Greenland.

Their monasteries stretched from the Bay of Biscay to Salzburg and Vienna and they even planted an Irish monastery in Kiev in Russia.

Perhaps these Irish Peregrini went further than we have yet realised. In 1982 an American archaeologist Robert Pyle photographed and traced a large petroglyph inscription in West Virginia, U.S.A. He sent his work to Dr. Barry Fell of Harvard, America's leading decipherer of ancient inscriptions. Fell immediately recognized the script as Ogam, the Celtic alphabet, and the language as Old Irish. The astounding message he translated was (in part), "The advent of the Saviour, Lord Christ, Behold, he is born of Mary, a woman." The ten foot long text speaks of the babe being born "in the cave of Bethlehem". And "Christmas is a happy season of joy and goodwill to all people."

The evidence from the style of writing dates the inscription somewhere during the Sixth to Ninth century.

Much more examination will be done. But we may ask ourselves whether we have stumbled on the tracks of some happy Perigrini Scoti following the long road that led them Home.

The high character and ability of the Peregrini became proverbial. An Irish pilgrim returning from the Holy Land was shipwrecked off Italy and the populace promptly elected him Bishop of Taranto. Donatus, another Irish pilgrim, was passing through Fiesole in north Italy in 829. The citizens were debating who to choose as bishop and they seized Donatus simply because he was a Peregrinus and made him bishop.

"Almost all of Ireland" said a ninth-century Bishop of Auxerre, "disregarding the ocean crossing, is migrating to our shores in a herd of philosophers." And the Abbot of Reichenau thought that the habit of becoming Peregrini was almost second nature to the Irish, adding "How can we forget Ireland, the island where the Sun of Faith arose for us?"

This massive and sustained campaign to win and teach Europe's motley population came just in time. During the century after the death of Columbanus in 615 AD the might of Islam swept across the world, conquering an empire from Samarkand to Gibraltar. Spain and the south of France fell to Muslim arms. Damascus blades and light cavalry were not the only cause of their astonishing conquests. In many lands which they overran, the inhabitants practiced the faith of their fathers only listlessly and were no match for the dedicated Arab believers. Islam filled a spiritual vacuum and won by default.

Charles Martel, leader of the Franks, defeated the Muslim host at Poitiers in 732 AD and halted their further conquest in France. But behind Martel stood a population newly united and strong in their Christian faith, thanks to the preaching monks from Ireland. Had it not been so, it

An I mo chridhe, I mo graidh
An ait guth manaich bidh
   geum ba
Ach mun tig an saoghal
   gu crich
Bithidh I mar a bha.

Iona of my heart,
   Iona of my love,
Instead of monks voices
   shall be the lowing of
   cattle;
But ere the world shall
   come to an end
Iona shall be as it was.

— Ancient Gaelic
prophesy attributed to
St. Columba.

Iona Abbey restored and alive.

seems quite likely that Rome might have gone the way of Jerusalem, Antioch and Alexandria.

Instead Rome sent forth an heroic missionary effort by the Benedictines. They matched the Irish in selfless dedication and brought to the alliance the classical learning and the Roman genius for order.

The Peregrini sketched the shape of Christendom on the face of Europe which began to take form during the reign of Charlemagne, Martel's grandson, an emperor who was devoted to their ideals. Perhaps it is not too much to say that the rise of Christendom was Ireland's gift to her neighbours.

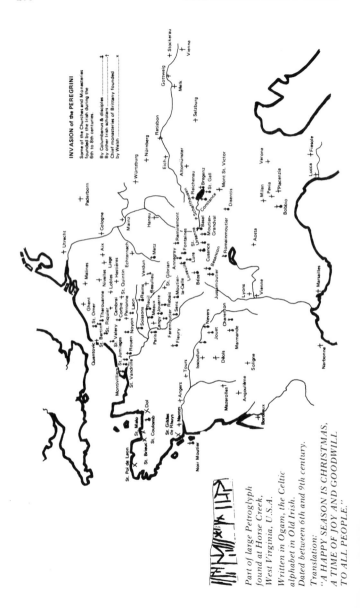

INVASION of the PEREGRINI

Some of the Churches and Monasteries
founded by the Irish during the
6th to 8th centuries.

By Columbanus & disciples ....
By other Irish scholars .... ✝
Chief monasteries of Brittany founded
by Welsh .... ✕

Part of large Petroglyph
found at Horse Creek,
West Virginia, U.S.A.

Written in Ogam, the Celtic
alphabet in Old Irish.
Dated between 6th and 9th century.

Translation:
"A HAPPY SEASON IS CHRISTMAS,
A TIME OF JOY AND GOODWILL
TO ALL PEOPLE."

A chapter of Columcille's story ends with the christening of the English and the invasion of Europe by the Peregrini. The grand strategy that had shaped his life was fulfilled and a new age had begun. The pivotal event had been the founding of Iona. Yet sad years lay ahead for his beloved island.

During the century-and-a-half when migrating barbarian hordes had cut the Celtic churches off from contact with Rome, they had remained part of the universal Church and there was no sign of schism. Attempts to depict them as in some way proto-protestant are ill informed. Although they had no Bishop Primate or central authority, it is remarkable that when they were again in touch with Rome there had been no divergence of doctrine. It says much for the purity of the Faith in Ireland — and in Rome. The only differences were an unusual hair style and an outdated method of computing Easter.

Yet unhappily these minor points, of no spiritual or moral importance, did cause friction. Celtic monks wore a tonsure which shaved the front of the head from ear to ear, letting the hair grow at the back. Probably it was copied from the *Filidh* when the Irish clergy became the new learned class. But during the years of separation the Roman clergy had adopted the coronal tonsure in memory of Our Lord's crown of thorns.

Computing the date of Easter had been a perpetual problem for the Church since the first century. In 541 AD at the Synod of Orleans new Easter Tables were adopted but in the chaos of the times no word of the change reached Ireland. But when communications were restored Rome had to insist that the clergy of the universal Church use the same identifying tonsure and the same date for Easter. Old habits die hard and the Celtic clergy would not conform.

In Northumbria the issue was quite a personal one for King Oswy and Queen Eanfled. She had been born on Easter Day and her father Edwin baptised on Easter, which she had always kept according to the Roman dating. But King Oswy, educated at Iona, followed the Celtic custom. At the Synod of Whitby in 664 AD Oswy and the Northumbrians accepted the Roman system.

Unfortunately Bishop Wilfred of York, who argued the Roman case, had spent much time in Gaul and picked up, it seems, some of the acrimony which had been directed against St. Columbanus. Wilfred won the argument but in such a way that the Iona missionaries felt slighted and they withdrew from England and many English monks went with them. They finally settled in the west of Ireland forming an English community in Mayo.

The Britons of Strathclyde and the Picts soon followed Northumbria's example and most of Ireland also accepted the new dating. But Iona clung to the old way.

The ninth Abbot of Iona was Adomnan macRonan and in 688 AD, after visiting Jarrow and talking to Bede's abbot Ceolfrid he accepted the Roman practice.

But many of the Iona monks refused to follow him, denouncing him, as a traitor to the Founder. It was this bitter controversy which led him to write his masterwork "The Life of St. Columba" to show his devotion to him. So perhaps we should be grateful.

After Adomnan died a faction at Iona set up a counter-Abbot and for decades there were two Abbots, two tonsures and two Easters on the island. Finally it was an Englishman, St. Egbert, who brought them to celebrate Easter together again in 729. Iona was the last Scottish abbey to conform.

Serious as was the Easter controversy, it must be viewed in perspective and it pales in importance against the mighty Celtic missionary surge which was occurring during this period. St. Maelrubha from Bangor founded his monastery at Applecross in 673, a light to all of northern Scotland. Peregrini were pouring into Europe, English bishops pushing boldly into Germany and Welsh missionaries doing magnificent work in Brittany and northern Spain. Iona itself had lavishly sent forth her most daring sons for more than a century. Small wonder if some of those who stayed behind were over-cautious men, more tenacious of tradition than of St. Columcille's worldwide vision.

Some have blamed Rome for the fading of Iona's importance but the real cause seems to have been the Viking terror. One day in 794 AD into the strait between Iona and Mull sailed the dragon ships and the sea was a protection no more. Iona, sacked three times, its Abbot and 68 monks massacred, was no longer tenable and the Brothers abandoned it, taking the Founder's relics with them. Some of the monks went to Kells in Ireland and some to Dunkeld in Scotland. The Abbots of Iona had always been chosen from Columcille's own clan in accordance with Celtic customs. The practice was continued at the new homes. Each Abbot of Dunkeld was also Chief of the Kindred of St. Columba in Scotland.

Columcille's body was taken to safety to Ireland but during the Viking raids there was no safe place and no one knows for certain where he was laid. If the old poem is true, he is buried at Downpatrick along with St. Patrick and St. Brigid.

> "His grace in God without stain
> And his soul in Derry,
> His body under the flagstone
> Where lie Brigid and Patrick."

But there is some doubt. In 1177 John de Courcy, the Norman adventurer, defeated MacDunlevy, the Irish king of Ulidia, and captured his capital Downpatrick. To help consolidate his grip on the captured kingdom, de Courcy restored and re-dedicated the church of the Holy Trinity at Down. He had the political good fortune to "discover" the bodies of Patrick, Bridget and Columcille which he re-buried with due pomp at the church. It gave de Courcy great prestige to have the graves of Ireland's three greatest saints. But it doesn't help the historians to accept it as authentic.

The Book of Durrow (c. 670) depicted St. Matthew apparently wearing the Celtic tonsure.

Chapter thirty-nine

Though the Celtic church and culture was wrecked by the Viking invasions, the Gaels triumphed in the end. They converted the Norsemen to Christianity and even Kings of Norway craved the honour of burial at holy Iona. The Kings of Alban continued to be buried there for it had become home for the heart of Pict and Scot alike. King Kenneth macAlpin, the half-Pictish Scot, who in 845 welded the two peoples together in the Kingdom of Alban, set his capital at Scone close to Dunkeld. He too lies in the soil of Iona.

But monasteries sacked time and again by sea-raiders, were rebuilt in stone with tall watch-towers. Yet to survive they had to have military protection. This is a reason why many Abbeys had an *erenagh*, a Lay Abbot, chosen from the Founder's Family, who undertook the armed protection and maintenance of the estates. Thus the clergy were freed for religious duties. The rank became hereditary and in time many an *erenagh* stood among the highest nobility.

Greatest of all in Scotland was the Lay Abbot of Dunkeld, Chief of the Kindred of Columba. His dangerous privilege was to ride at the head of the Scottish battle array, carrying *Cathbuaidh*, Battle Victory, St. Columba's crozier. It led the battleline at Strathearn in 905 when King Constantin slew the Dane Ua Imhair, it saw victory at Tynemoor in 916 and Abbot Duncan fell carrying it in 964.

Crinan, probably Duncan's grandson, was Lay Abbot and Chief of the Kindred when he married Bethoc, daughter of King Malcolm II. Their son Duncan ascended the throne as King of Scots in 1034 and thus Columba's own clan became the Royal Family of the nation that he had done so much to bring to birth.

It was at this time that the red, ramping lion, totem animal of the Cenel Conaill of Donegal, Columba's clan, replaced the Boar of Dalriada as the royal beast of Scotland.

Malcolm Canmore, Duncan's son, and his English wife St. Margaret, solidified the Kingdom. They restored the Abbey at Iona and the Chapel of Relieg Oran is thought to date from their time. Their gifted sons, especially David, built a national fabric which withstood the shocks of time and established Scotland's boundries much as they are today.

Robert Bruce, Norman by name but descended from David through his grandmother, was the last King of Scots to carry Columba's relics into battle. The reliquary, called *Brecbennoch* now in the Museum of Antiquaries, Edinburgh, was trooped through the Scottish ranks on the morning of the epic victory of Bannockburn.

Many clans and Families claim descent from the Kindred of Columba. The Royal Family, Bruce, MacDuff, Robertson, Cummins, Wemyss, Carlyle, Home, Dundas to name a few. Chiefs of the Clans Macdonald, MacDougall, MacKinnon, MacLean, MacNaughten, MacLaghlan, display in their Arms the heraldic symbol of the Kindred — a hand holding a Triune Cross.

The Gaels have cherished the memory of the missionaries of Columban times and the names of the "sacred families" show it. Priests of those days married as Ministers do today.

Gilles	— servant of Jesus
Malise	— devotee of Jesus
Gilchrist	— servant of Christ
Gilmore	— servant of Mary
Morrison	— servant of Mary
MacLean	— servant of John
MacRae	— son of Grace
MacBeth	— son of Life
Malcolm	— devotee of Columba
Gillanders	— servant of Andrew
MacPherson	— son of the Parson
MacTaggart	— son of the Priest
MacMillan	— son of tonsured one
MacNab	— son of the Abbot
Buchanan	— house of Canon
Gillespie	— servant of Bishop
Dewar	— keeper of a sacred relic

Popular memory gave Columba the predominant place in Scotland's early Christian history and it is sad that too little regard is paid to the contributions of Ninian and Mungo. But it is due to the accident of history which gave to the Gaelic Scots the chief role in uniting the peoples of Scotland. Kenneth MacAlpin and his dynasty revered Ninian and Mungo as mighty men of God, but Columba was a Gael, a prince of their own blood, their very own saint. Because of Lindisfarne the Northumbrians thought of him as their own apostle. When Duncan, son of a Chief of the Kindred, came to the throne, he naturally regarded his saintly kinsman as special patron of his realm.

It therefore seems strange that Columba is not the Patron Saint of Scotland. How did that happen?

There are many legends about how St. Andrew became Patron but probably what happened was this. The first missionaries to England from Rome came from Pope

Gregory's monastery of St. Andrew's. Therefore this Saint was specially venerated by the English. Hexham Abbey in Northumbria was dedicated to him.

Bede's friend Acca was Bishop of Hexham from 709 to 732. He had brought back from Rome a precious relic of St. Andrew which was solemnly enshrined in Hexham cathedral. But then Acca was driven into exile and fled to the Picts for sanctuary, taking the relic with him. He settled in the monastery of Kilrymont in Fife and never returned to Hexham. Here at his new home the relic was enshrined and the Brethren changed the name of their church to St. Andrews.

Because their church now had the only relic of one of the Apostles in Scotland, great prestige and status came to them. St. Andrews became the premier bishopric. And from 750 St. Andrew was venerated as the Patron Saint of Scotland. This was just the period when Iona was in bad standing with the Kings of the Picts because of the Easter controversy.

Scots tend to think of Columba as a Scottish saint who happened to be born in Ireland. The Irish are sure Columcille is an Irish saint who did do some work in Scotland! Of course, they are both right. He is Ireland's hero and greatest son. And he is Scotland's saint of saints and founding father of the nation. He left us a vision of what God can do through a wholehearted man and that vision can still stir the blood of the Gael to dare the impossible.

Brecbennoch, containing St. Columba's relics was borne before the Scottish army at Bannockburn, 1314. In National Museum of Antiquities, Edinburgh.

Ranald, Lord of the Isles and name-father of the Macdonalds of Clanranald, staffed Iona with monks of St. Benedict's Order. They completely rebuilt the Abbey Church much as it appears today and added the Nunnery for the Nuns of their Order, whose Abbess was Bethoc, Ranald's sister. This was about 1200. Ranald's finely carved grave stone can still be seen at the Abbey. Iona once again was a place of light and learning. And so it remained — sometimes more and sometimes less — until the Reformation.

At Iona there was no statue-smashing by over-zealous Reformers, although some of the 300 standing crosses may have been pitched into the sea. But frost, rain and neglect slowly crumbled the Abbey into ruins. And Columcille's prophecy came true:

> "Iona of my heart, Iona of my love,
> Instead of monks' voices there shall be lowing of cattle."

Yet even in decay Iona retained its attraction. One dark October evening in 1773 two most unlikely pilgrims arrived. They had to be carried ashore from the boat because there was no longer a landing dock and they slept on hay in a barn. Iona must have seemed to them as remote as Greenland. Yet to Dr. Samuel Johnson, the noted man of letters, and his Scottish friend Boswell it was the one place in Scotland they most wanted to see.

No church or school survived on Holy Iona but even in its total desolation it stirred their minds. "That man is little to be envied whose piety would not grow warmer among the ruins of Iona," wrote Johnson, adding with prophetic insight "Sometime again it may be the instructress of the Western regions."

Samuel Johnson's visit focussed the interest of cultured men in Europe. Many came exploring, as did Sir Walter Scott, Keats and Wordsworth, and in 1829 Felix Mendelssohn. When he returned to Germany his sisters asked him to tell them about Iona. "It cannot be told" he replied, "It can only be played" and sitting down at the piano he played what became the "Overture to the Hebrides."

The Royal Yatch sailed into the Sound in 1847 with Queen Victoria and Prince Albert aboard. The Prince went ashore to pay his homage among the grass-grown tombstones of the Kings in the Releig Oran. The Royal interest breathed new life into the Island. An hotel was built and in summer a steamer came daily from Oban.

The Dukes of Argyll, Chiefs of Clan Campbell, had owned the Island for 300 years. The 8th Duke in 1899 made a gift of the ruined Abbey to the Church of Scotland on condition it be restored and open to worshippers of all Denominations. By 1910 the Abbey Church had risen again and prayer and hymns rose anew under its roof.

Now came what may be called "the third founding of Iona". It started during the "hungry 1930s" of the Depression. A Minister, the Rev. George MacLeod, in the poorest district of Glasgow, was troubled that while he preached from the pulpit about the Bread of Life, unemployed workmen in the pews did not have enough bread for a decent breakfast. Somehow these two realities must be resolved.

From this seed thought grew the Iona Community, a brotherhood of laymen and clergy seeking together to "forge a new vocabulary of work and worship". George MacLeod thought of the grass covered walls of Iona's monastery, forlornly surrounding the restored Abbey Church. Here at Scotland's most sacred site was work needing to be done. Where better for the Community to work out its experiment? For here they would not only restore an historic fabric but seek to rekindle the revolutionary Christian experience that had brought Columcille and his men over the sea to Scotland. So the workmen built the walls and the clergy worked beside them. And when the clergy prayed in the Abbey, the workmen knelt beside them.

By the summer of 1939 they had raised the walls of the old Chapter House and Library. It was urgent to get a weather-tight roof on before the winter storms.

But in September the Second World War broke out. All building supplies were commandeered for the War Effort. There was no timber for the roof, no hope of obtaining any. The Community did the only thing they could do — and what Columcille would have done. They prayed.

Far out in the Atlantic a Norwegian freighter sailed homeward with a deck cargo of Canadian lumber. During a howling gale the cargo broke loose and went overboard. It drifted eastward. It missed Ireland and the Outer Hebrides, finally washing ashore on the coast of Mull, directly opposite Iona Abbey. The Community was quick to salvage it and found to their amazement that it was precisely the type of lumber they needed, precisely the amount they needed and it was even cut to the right lengths. So the Library got its roof and the word CAN-ADA can still be read on some of the beams.

One day during the War the tide washed ashore the body of an unknown British seaman. The islanders debated where he should be buried and they agreed it would be fitting that he should lie, not in the village graveyard, but among the Kings and Chiefs in the Releig Oran. Some time later the body of a German Luftwaffe airman, washed ashore. Again it was decided that this stranger should be buried beside the seaman.

Islanders served as his pall bearers and one who had a trumpet sounded the Last Post as Dr. George MacLeod committed the body to the grave.

Dr. MacLeod wrote "After the War quite miraculously we discovered who this poor fellow was and I was able to write and tell his family that he was buried in Royal ground. They were profoundly touched and grateful." The words of the ancient Gaelic "Song of Hospitality" come to mind:

"And the lark said in her song
    Often, often, often
Goes Christ in the stranger's guise."

George MacLeod became Moderator of the Church of Scotland and the Rt. Rev. Lord MacLeod. When in London, he was searching for a Cross suitable for the main altar of the Abbey. In a small shop he saw a beautiful silver Cross but the shop-keeper refused to sell it to him. She said — "My husband was a silversmith and this is the last thing he made. Before he died he told me he intended it for the altar of Iona's Abbey." Lord MacLeod explained who he was and that this was the very purpose he wanted the Cross. So the silversmith's last wish came true.

It is not possible in this book to give even a brief outline of the work done by the Iona Community, on and off the Island, during the last forty years.

A century ago, Iona stood ruined and lifeless. But now prayer and praise sound again in the Abbey. The Bread and Wine are consecrated by clergy of many Confessions — "the holy men of other churches" that Columba foretold would come. In the Refectory there is again the smell of cooking and the clatter of dishes. In the Cloisters groups of jean-clad youngsters debate how history may be turned right side up. And the pilgrims come again by thousands from all around the globe. Some come merely "because Iona was on the Tour"; other come hoping to find the secret of "the kind Columcille". And week by week there are those who find it. And a tourist becomes a pilgrim. Iona is alive.

That is the measure of what George MacLeod and the Iona Community have brought about. Like the Island Soldiers before them, they dared to believe in miracles and they have not been disappointed.

Chapter forty-one

Our search for Columcille has taken us from his birth-place in Donegal to his "place of resurrection" as monks called it, at Iona. We have walked with him and heard his words, watched him at work in youth and old age. We know his comrades and his opponents and something of his world. He is no longer a stranger.

As a young man we saw him deliberately reject a life of power, riches and ambition and we have traced the work-ing out of that decision, mapping the course of his unwavering purpose in his statesmanship. This was no egocentric recluse escaping in remorse to a distant island. We can lay that myth to rest.

No historical evidence supports the charge of vindic-tiveness and violence. And the tale of exile is misinformed. As to "meddling in politics", as a prince and adviser to kings, he was inevitably concerned with politics. His work resulted in far-ranging political, social and eco-nomic consequences. But the important point is to note how he operated in the political sphere.

Without doubt he and Bishop Mungo cemented together the Christian alliance which triumphed at the battle of Ardderyd. But how did they do it? Not by political means but by spiritual. Before they put the Kings Brude, Rhydderch and Maelgwn in touch with each other, they first put them in touch with God. Their politics were to change the hearts of politicians. And that is the true mis-sion of priests.

Around Columcille most of his life swirled the great war of faiths, deciding the shape of the future for Ireland

and Britain. The victory of the Christian cause was first won in the courageous lives of Columcille and his friends, — the Twelve Apostles of Ireland and men like Cadoc, David and Mungo among the Britons.

The Ireland of his boyhood was still largely pagan and illiterate. Before he died it was already becoming famous in Europe as the land of saints and scholars. Yet the ancient oral wisdom of the Celts had been preserved.

The ideal hero of the Irish of old was the mighty warrior Cuchulain whose trophies were the heads of his neighbours. Columcille personified a new ideal, a selfless man who freed his neighbours from sickness and want, fear and vengeance, and the Irish took this new hero to their hearts as a Christian Cuchulain. Their hearts were his trophies.

The founding of Iona stands out like a divine intervention in history. It was the decisive stroke in the war of faiths and it let loose the spirit of the Peregrini which transformed Europe.

This little rocky island is the *Lia Fail,* the Stone of Destiny on which our race was founded. It drew the northern tribes together and gave Scotland a soul before she even had a name. It led the English into a new destiny. So the date of Iona's founding, 563 AD, may be regarded as the most significant date for the English-speaking peoples of the world.

We have come to know our first knowable ancestor —this Irish prince, pilgrim, poet and sailor, "the kind Columcille". A fig-tree bearing a rich harvest. By this fruit let him be judged.

We are his heirs, kindred of the magnificent Gael of Iona.

INDEX

C

D

H

I

J

K

L

M

N

O

P

REFERENCES AND NOTES

p. 2   Columcille is pronounced with a hard C, like a K.

p. 6   Bishop Finbar, "white head", of Moville (d. ca.579) was
         also called Finnian. In this book he is called Finbar to
         avoid confusion with St. Finnian of Clonard. There was
         also a St. Finbar of Cork but he does not come into the
         narrative.

p. 8   Adomnan's Life of Columba, A.O. & M.O. Anderson.
         Introduction p. 3.
         Early Christian Ireland: introduction to sources. Kathleen
         Hughes. p. 224.

p. 9   St. Patrick: Davis Lectures 1958. Ludwig Bieler. p. 53.

p. 16   Celtic Heritage. A. & B. Rees. p. 55.

p. 19   Everyday Life of Pagan Celts. Anne Ross. p. 76.

p. 30   King Arthur's Avalon. G. Ashe. p. 55.

p. 40   Celtic Scotland, Vol. II. W.F. Skene. p. 50.

p. 37   This brief summary of monastic training is chiefly based
         on Irish Monasticism, Section III. John Ryan.

p. 46   Rats, Lice & History. H. Zinsser. p. 106.

p. 50   Bede, Vol. II. Book I. Ch. XIV.

p. 56   Celtic Realms. M. Dillon & N. Chadwick. p. 112.
         King Arthur's Avalon. G. Ashe. p. 77.
         There are two sites favoured as the location of the battle
         of Mount Badon: Badbury Rings in Dorset and Liddington
         Castle near Swindon. The early *Annales Cambriae* date
         the battle in 516: Bede dates it in 490.

p. 59   Celtic Scotland, Vol. II. W.F. Skene. p. 179.

p. 65   Irish Monasticism. J. Ryan. p. 298.

p. 67   Ireland Before the Vikings. G. MacNiocaill. p. 26.

p. 68   Celtic Scotland. Vol. II. W.F. Skene. p. 82.

p. 67   St. Columba of Iona. L. Menzies. p. 91.
         At tne end of the Durrow Gospels, transcribed in the 7th
         century from an original now lost, is written: "I pray thy
         blessedness, O Holy presbyter St. Patrick, that whosoever
         shall take this book into his hands may remember the
         writer Columba. I wrote this gospel for my own use in
         the space of 12 days, by the grace of God."

p. 75   Early Christian Ireland: introduction to sources.
         K. Hughes. p. 71.

p. 78   Early Christian Ireland: intro. to sources. K. Hughes.
         p. 72.
         Irish Kings and High Kings. F.J. Byrne. p. 110.

p. 81   The *Dearg druchtach* is mentioned in a poem "Columcille
         Cecenit" attributed to the saint. It also speaks of Cormac
         O'Lethan being at Durrow. But he did not become Prior
         of Durrow till after 580 so the poem must be after that
         date. There are two verses in the middle of the poem
         which imply that it was written at the time Columcille
         "went into exile". But they appear to be clumsy additions
         made later by someone obsessed with the myth of the
         "exile". They are completely out of tune with the rest of
         the poem which reads as a unity without them.

p. 108   Opinions vary about St. Kentigern founding Llanelwy.
         Welsh scholars like Sir John Edward Lloyd and Sir Ifor
         Evans accept it; others do not. On balance the evidence
         seems to support it.

p. 118   Ireland before the Vikings. B. MacNiocaill. p. 77.
         Kings and Kingship in Early Scotland. M.O. Anderson. p.
         149.
         Irish Dalriada was small, about thirty miles from north to
         south and fifteen miles wide. But strategically it controlled
         the North Channel, the shortest route to Scotland.

p. 122   Irish Kings and High Kings, F.J. Byrne. p. 111.
         Columcille is said to have warned Aidan of disaster if he
         or his heirs broke this compact with the Ui Neill of
         Ailech. One historian termed this "spiritual blackmail".
         However, Aidan's grandson Domnall Breac, who had a
         talent for disaster, did break the compact, attacking the Ui
         Neill in 637 and so lost the Irish lands of Dalriada. Later
         he quarrelled with the Britons of Strathclyde who killed
         him in battle in 642. His death marked the end of the
         Scot-Irish kingdom of Dalriada. It seems that Columcille
         demonstrated, not blackmail, but good political foresight.
         A fable claimed that Columcille, being "in perpetual
         exile", attended Druim Ceatt with a blanket over his head
         so that he should not see Ireland and with a turf of
         Scottish soil tied on each foot so that he should not walk
         on Irish soil. It is a tale for fairy books.

p. 154   The Arms of the City of Glasgow display a tree, a bird, a
         bell and a salmon holding a ring in its mouth — all
         symbols associated with St. Mungo. These elements have

been used by the Diocese and City since the dawn of
heraldry, but a Patent of Arms was only granted by Lord
Lyon as recently as 1866. The Crest is the figure of St.
Mungo, hand raised in blessing. Pope Gregory's cross may
have been the gold pectoral cross which was treasured for
centuries at the Columban monastery on Tory Island off
the north-west coast of Ireland. It passed into the custody
of the MacDonnells of Dunluce. In 1584 Queen Elizabeth's
Deputy for Ireland, Sir John Perrot, stormed Dunluce
castle. Among the booty was St. Columba's pectoral cross
which Sir John sent with a facetious note to a lady friend
in London. The note survives in the Elizabethan state
papers but the fate of the cross is unknown.

See "Rathlin—Disputed Island" by Wallace Clark, 1971.

p. 159   Prebendary W. Carlile, D.H., D.D. (1847-1942). Founder of
the Church Army. Buried in St. Paul's Cathedral, London.

p. 185   Edwin had previously ravaged the lands of the Britons in
Anglesey, sufficient cause to enrage the Island Dragon.

CHRONOLOGY

A.D.

43	Roman Emperor Claudius conquered Britain.
67	St. Peter and St. Paul martyred at Rome.
123	Emperor Hadrian built Wall across Britain.
285	St. Antony of Egypt withdrew to Desert, founder of monasticism.
306	Constantine the Great proclaimed Emperor at York.
313	Edict of Milan granted religious toleration.
367	Great Raid of Picts, Saxons and Scots overran Britain.
c370	Nine cohorts of Britaniciani Juniores enlisted from north Britons.
372	St. Martin founded Magis Monasterium at Tours.
378	Goth cavalry annihilated Legions, killed eastern Emperor at Adrianople.
383	Magnus Maximus, proclaimed at York, became Augustus of the West; took Legions to Gaul, killed 388.
c390	Cunedda, with British cohorts, drove Scoti out of north Wales, founded kingdom of Gwynedd.
397	St. Ninian founded Candida Casa at Whithorn. Death of St. Martin of Tours.
405?	St. Patrick kidnapped by Irish slave traders.
410	Visigoths sacked Rome. Legions left Britain.
425	Vortigern governed Britons. Pelagian heresy.
429	Bishop Germanus of Auxerre went to Britain to refute heresy. Won "Alleluia Victory" over Picts and Saxons.
432?	St. Patrick sent to Ireland as Bishop.
444	Plague swept Britain. Vortigern recruited Saxon mercenaries. Hengist and Horsa to drive back Picts.
452	Attila the Hun invaded Italy.
455	Vandals sacked Rome.
461?	Death of St. Patrick.
c480	Britons, under Ambrosius, won a prosperous respite.
496	King Clovis of the Franks converted.
500	Fergus macErc with brothers Lorn and Angus founded Scots of Dalriada in Argyll. Cerdic the West Saxon landed at Southampton.
c500	St. Illtud taught at Llanilltud, S. Wales.
516	Arthur led Britons to victory in a dozen battles, ending at Mount Badon. 20 years of peace. St. Gildas born at Strathclyde.
521	St. Columba born at Gartan, Donegal, Ireland.
525	System of dating from AD adopted.
529	St. Benedict founded monastery of Monte Cassino, Italy.

537	Arthur killed at battle of Camlann.
535	Emperor Justinian briefly reunited East and West Empire.
c540	St. Finnian taught "Twelves Apostles of Ireland" at Clonard.
541	Council of Orleans adopted new dating system for Easter.
c546	King Rhydderch, Bishop Mungo, St. Gildas driven from Strathclyde into exile by pagan revival.
	Ostrogoths sacked Rome.
548	Yellow Plague.
	Death of St. Ciaran of Clonmacnois, St. Finnian of Clonard.
549	St. Columba founded monastery of Derry.
554	St. Comgall founded Bangor.
c560	St. Gildas wrote "De Excidio".
	St. Mungo founded monastery of Llanelwy in N. Wales.
561	Battle of Culdremne.
563	St. Columba founded monastery at Iona.
	Fall of Tara.
	2nd outbreak of Yellow Plague. Death of King Maelgwn of Gwynedd.
565	Columba, Comgall and Kenneth converted Brude, High King of Picts.
568	Lombards conquered Italy.
570	Prophet Mohammed born.
573	Battle of Ardderyd. Bishop Mungo recalled to Strathclyde.
574	Aidan consecrated King of Scots by St. Columba.
575	Convention of Druim Ceatt.
577	Battle of Dyrham. West Saxons broke through to Bristol channel.
584	Death of Brude, High King of Picts.
585	King Aidan won battle against Maeatae Picts and Saxons, St. Columba visited St. Mungo at Glasgow. A combined campaign to convert southern Picts. St. Kenneth founded Kilrymont (St. Andrews).
c590	St. Mungo visited Pope Gregory in Rome. Pope's seven emisaries travelled to Iona.
	St. Columbanus left Bangor to begin his mission to Europe.
597	Death of St. Columba at Iona.
	St. Augustine landed in Kent to begin conversion of English.
600	Death of St. Comgall of Bangor, St. Baithen of Iona.
603	Death of King Rhydderch and St. Mungo.
	Battle of Dawstane; Aidan defeated by Ethelfrid of Northumbria.
616	Ethelfrid captured Chester, cutting Wales off from Strathclyde.
617	Ethelfrid killed. His sons Oswald and Oswy sought sanctuary at Iona.

627   King Edwin of Northumbria with his people baptised by
        Bishop Paulinus and Bishop Rhun.
633   King Edwin killed by Penda of Mercia.
        Oswald returned from Iona, defeated Cadwalla at
        Heavenfield, became King of Northumbria.
635   Bishop Aidan sent from Iona to help Oswald convert his
        people.
        Founded Lindisfarne, "a second Iona".
642   Oswald killed at Oswestry, succeeded by Oswy.
664   Synod of Whitby decided to adopt Roman dating for Easter.
688   Abbot Adomnan of Iona wrote "Life of St. Columba".

BIBLIOGRAPHY

ALCOCK, Leslie — Arthur's Britain, 1973, Allen Lane, Penguin Press.

ANDERSON, A.O. — Adomnan's Life of Columba, 1961, Nelson & Sons, London.

ASHE, Geoffrey — Quest for Arthur's Britain, 1972 edition.

BEDE, Venerable — Church History of the English People, 1974 edition, Penguin Books Ltd.

BOWEN, E.G. — Saints, Seaways and Settlements, 1969, University of Wales Press.

BRODSTED, Johannes — The Vikings, 1970, Penguin Books Ltd.

BYRNE, Francis J. — Irish Kings and High Kings, 1973, B.T. Batsford, London.

CHADWICK, Nora — The Celts, 1971, Cox & Wyman, London.

DILLON & CHADWICK — Celtic Realms, 1947, MacMillan Co., New York

GITS, Rev. Alex — Life of St. Mungo, 1967, Burns & Sons, Glasgow.

GREEN, A.S. — History of the Irish State before 1014.

HENDERSON, Isabel — The Picts, 1967, Thames & Hudson, London.

HUGHES, Kathleen — Early Christian Ireland: introduction to the sources, 1972, Hodder & Stoughton Ltd.

MENZIES, Lucy — St. Columba of Iona, 1920 and 1970 editions, J.M. Dent & Sons, London.

MELDRUN, E. — Dark Ages in the Highlands, 1971, Inverness Field Club.

MONCRIEFFE, Sir Iain — The Highland Clans, 1967, Bremball House, New York.

MORRISON, John — Behold Iona, 1963, Iona Community Publishing Dept., Glasgow.

MOODY, T.W. and MARTIN, F.X. — Course of Irish History, 1965, Mercer Press, Cork.

MacEVEDY, Colin — Atlas of Ancient History, 1972, Penguin Books Ltd.

McNEILL, John T. — The Celtic Churches, 1974, University of Chicago Press.

MacNIOCAILL, Gearoid — Ireland Before the Vikings, 1972, Gill & MacMillan Ltd., Dublin.

RICHMOND, I.A. — Roman Britain, 1963, Penguin Books Ltd.

ROSS, Anne   Everyday Life of the Pagan Celts, 1970,
                                 B.T. Batsford Ltd., London.

ROSS, John M.   Scottish History and Literature, 1884.

RYAN, John   Irish Monasticism, 1931, Talbot Press
                                 Ltd., Dublin.

SKENE, W.F.   Celtic Scotland, Vols. I, II, III, 1886,
                                 David Douglas, Edinburgh.

THOMAS, Charles   Britain and Ireland in Early Christian
                                 times, 1971, McGraw Hill Co., New
                                 York.